the Crockery Cook

Mable Hoffman

FISHER BOOKS™
er

Publishers:	Bill Fisher
	Helen Fisher
	Howard Fisher
Editor:	Helen Fisher
Managing Editor:	Sarah Trotta
Production & Design:	Anne Olson, Casa Cold Type, Inc.
Production Manager:	Deanie Wood
Illustrations:	Image Club Graphics © 1996

Published by

Fisher Books
4239 W. Ina Road
Tucson, AZ 85741

Library of Congress Cataloging-in-Publication Data

Hoffman, Mable, 1922-

[Mable Hoffman's all new crockery favorites]

The crockery cook / Mable Hoffman.

p. cm.

Rev. ed of: Mable Hoffman's all-new crockery favorites / by Mable & Gar Hoffman. 1991

Includes index.

ISBN 1-55561-155-9

1. Electric cookery, Slow. 2. Casserole cookery. I. Hoffman, Mable, 1922- Mable Hoffman's all-new crockery favorites.

II. Title.

TX827.H57 1998

641.5' 884--dc21   98-24611

CIP

Notice: The information in this book is true and complete to the best of our knowledge. It is offered with no guarantees on the part of the author or Fisher Books. Author and publisher disclaim all liability with use of this book.

Featured on the cover is the Rival® Crock-Pot® Slow Cooker. The Rival Crock-Pot is a registered trademark of The Rival Co.

Contents

About the Author

Twenty-three years ago, Mable Hoffman, with husband Gar, began a collaboration with the Fishers in developing recipes for slow cookers. This collaboration resulted in *Crockery Cookery*, a best-selling cookbook that has remained available throughout the years and still enjoys widespread appeal. Then followed *Crockery Favorites* as a companion book with new recipes, menus and ideas.

The Hoffmans became Fisher Books' best-selling cookbook team and, in addition to *Crockery Favorites*, have a long list of successful cookbooks, including *Ice Cream, Frozen Yogurt* and *Carefree Entertaining*. Five of Mable's cookbooks have won R.T. French Tastemaker Awards for cookbooks.

Mable Hoffman owns and manages Hoffman Food Consultants, Inc., where she concentrates her efforts on food styling, recipe development and writing. She has traveled worldwide gathering ideas and information about foods and cuisines.

Documentation

Nutrient analysis was calculated using The Food Processor II Nutrition & Diet Analysis System software program, version 3.0, copyright 1988, 1990 by ESHA Research. Analysis does not include optional ingredients. Where a range of servings is provided, analysis is done using the higher number.

Abbreviations

Because words like **carbohydrates** are too long to fit in chart form, the following abbreviations are used:

Cal = Calories   Prot = Protein   Carb = Carbohydrate   Chol = Cholesterol

Menus

Susie's Bean Dish, page 2
Cole Slaw
Cornbread
Orange-Date Pudding, page 3

Chinese Braised Chicken, page 22
Steamed Rice with Peas
Marinated Sliced Cucumbers
Tomato Wedges
Jicama and Bell Pepper Strips
Fresh Pineapple Slices
Ginger-Pear Sherbet

Savory Turkey Chowder, page 48
Sliced Tomatoes
Celery and Zucchini Sticks
French Bread
Peppermint Ice Cream
Brownies

Tamale Soup, page 64
Mixed Green Salad
Tortillas
Flan
Coconut Macaroons

Crockery Cassoulet, page 109
Fresh Mushroom Salad
French Bread
Apple Tart

Broiled Fish
Southwestern Sauce, page 113
Spaghetti Squash
Green Salad
Blue Corn Muffins
Piña Colada Bread Pudding, page 45

Barbecued Beef Sandwiches, page 126
French Rolls
Corn on the Cob
Traditional Baked Beans, page 65
Rhubarb Pie

Sunshine Drumsticks, page 139
Tossed Green Salad
Mixed Vegetables
Whole-wheat Muffins
Chocolate Cake

Antipasto Bean Salad, page 128
Flank Steak Pinwheels, page 77
Noodles with Poppy Seeds
Ginger Carrots
Zucchini Muffins

Crockery Cooking

Crockery cooking is almost like having a cook at home fixing dinner while you're involved in other activities. It's nice to come home to a kitchen full of enticing aromas and a meal ready to eat. Hearty family-style fare, as well as special occasion dishes, can be cooked while you are away.

For safe and enjoyable cooking, here are a few tips to remember before using your slow cooker:

➤ Read and follow the manufacturer's "Use and Care" booklet that comes with your cooker.

➤ There are two temperature levels on most slow cookers: LOW or 200F (95C) and HIGH or 300F (150C).

➤ It's best to use LOW when leaving a cooker unattended.

➤ If you're home, and need to cook a little faster, turn the control to HIGH for the last hour or two of cooking.

➤ Don't lift the lid on a slow cooker while it's cooking. Because the temperature is extremely low, heat quickly escapes when the lid is removed, thus requiring even longer cooking time.

➤ It isn't necessary to stir food while cooking.

➤ For easier cleanup, use vegetable cooking spray or grease the interior of your slow cooker before adding ingredients.

Crockery Cooking Basics

Heat Comes from Sides of Pot

Unlike pots and pans you use on your stovetop, most slow cookers heat from the sides instead of the bottom. Heating coils are in the outside metal shell holding the liner. When you turn it on, these coils become hot and heat the crockery liner. Others use a heating base that provides heat from the bottom. For best results, the pot should be at least half-full of ingredients.

Amount of Liquid

If you're a novice at slow cooking, you'll notice more liquid in the pot at the end of cooking than with traditional cooking methods. With a lower cooking temperature, liquids do not boil away and vegetables and meats are not likely to dry out. As a result, most recipes call for the addition of far less liquids.

High-altitude Cooking

Most foods take longer to cook at high altitudes. If you live in a high-altitude area, plan on a longer cooking time.

Root Vegetables

Dense vegetables such as carrots, turnips, celery root, potatoes, onions and rutabagas, take longer to cook than many meats. When combining ingredients in a slow cooker, place root vegetables on the bottom of the pot, then add meats, seasonings, other vegetables and liquid. This keeps vegetables moist during cooking and cooks them more evenly.

Dried Beans

Cooking time for dried beans varies with the specific bean as well as the ingredients cooked with them. In general, small white beans, great Northern and baby limas take much less cooking time than kidney beans and garbanzos.

In some cases, certain beans should be cooked on HIGH instead of LOW. Presoaking beans before cooking them in a slow cooker is not usually necessary, but it shortens the cooking time.

Check recipes for specific directions.

Pasta and Rice

These products are at their best when cooked according to traditional methods or microwaved, then added to slow-cooked recipes near the end of the cooking time. If cooked for many hours, they become gummy or fall apart.

Dairy Products

Dairy products are delicious additions to many recipes but, in most cases, should be added to the slow cooker near the end of the cooking time. Milk usually separates

and looks curdled when cooked for hours. There are a few exceptions where milk products are mixed in with other ingredients and successfully slow-cooked.

Seasonings

Additional salt has been omitted from recipes that call for ingredients which contain salt. Experiment with using larger amounts of spices because slow cooking produces more liquid, diluting the effect of your spices.

Advantages of Slow Cooking

Food Cooks While You Are Away

Cooking with LOW heat does not dry out or burn the food. Put everything in the pot, cover and cook on LOW. You can leave for the day and dinner will be ready when you return.

Exact Timing Is Not Crucial

If you're delayed getting home, another half hour or hour of cooking time doesn't make much difference to most recipes that are cooking on LOW. The temperature is so low that exact timing is not critical.

Saves Energy

You benefit because this is a cost-efficient method of meal preparation. Crockery pots use very little electricity because the wattage is low.

Ease of Preparation

Prepare vegetables and other cut-up ingredients the day before. Wrap and refrigerate separately until needed.

Does Not Heat the Kitchen

Although crockery cooking is associated with hearty winter dishes, this book offers many year-round recipe suggestions to help you keep your kitchen cool all summer.

Foods Are Moist and Flavorful

Inexpensive cuts of meat benefit greatly from slow cooking because the usual shrinkage is prevented. While slow cooking, meat and vegetable juices blend together, creating more flavorful dishes.

Handy for Buffets

Prepare appetizers or main dishes in the slow cooker. Keep the pot plugged in on LOW, and the food will be just as warm for the last guest as it was for the first.

You Can Take It with You

When going to a potluck or picnic in the park, prepare a main dish or vegetable at home. To transport it, wrap the entire hot, filled slow cooker with lid in place in two layers of foil, then at least five layers of newspaper. Secure wrappings with tape. Place wrapped cooker upright in a small box. Keep in upright position at all times.

Thickening Sauces and Gravy

Flavorful juices left in the pot after slow cooking meats and vegetables are another plus of crockery cooking. There are several ways to thicken these juices, then you can use them as sauces to enhance the food.

Juices are usually thickened after the meat and vegetables have been removed with a slotted spoon. In some cases, the juices can be thickened while the meat and/or vegetables are in the pot. Each recipe indicates the exact proportion for a specific sauce.

Following are some general guidelines.

Cornstarch

When food is cooked, turn slow cooker on HIGH. Dissolve cornstarch in a cup with an equal amount of water. Stir into pot juices. Cover and cook on HIGH 20 to 30 minutes, stirring occasionally, until thickened. Use 2 tablespoons cornstarch dissolved in 2 tablespoons cold water to thicken about 2 cups liquid.

Flour

Follow the procedure above for cornstarch. But note that the amount of flour and water are different. Use 4 tablespoons flour dissolved in 4 tablespoons water to create a medium sauce with 2 cups liquid.

Quick-cooking Tapioca

This is stirred into liquid in the slow cooker before cooking. It thickens as the meat and vegetables cook. With 2 cups liquid, add 3 or 4 tablespoons quick-cooking tapioca.

Vegetables

In certain recipes, mashed beans are used to thicken mixtures. In other recipes, potato flakes or puréed potatoes are used with other vegetables.

Enhancing Presentation

➤ At serving time, sprinkle top with chopped fresh herbs, chopped tomatoes, green onions, grated cheese, buttered crumbs or crushed corn chips.

➤ For a stew-type dish, drop mounds of dumpling batter on top of cooked mixture; cover and cook on HIGH 30 to 45 minutes. *See page 145.*

➤ Spoon cooked-meat mixture into scooped-out French rolls; over toasted English muffins; in puffed pastry shells; in crisp taco shells; over soft flour tortillas; in pita rounds; over cornbread squares; over cooked fettuccine or other pasta; over cooked regular, brown or wild rice; over baked potatoes.

➤ Cook meat or chicken with seasonings in slow cooker a day ahead. Refrigerate overnight. Place in casserole. Cover with your favorite pastry recipe, refrigerated biscuits or ready-to-bake pie crust; bake according to package directions.

➤ Add pea pods, mushrooms and other quick-cooking vegetables near the end of cooking time.

Browning

It's not necessary to brown food before slow cooking, and this procedure is not indicated in recipes in this book. Generally, food prepared in a slow cooker doesn't brown as it does in a skillet or oven.

However, if you prefer the color and flavor of browned meat, poultry, onions or other vegetables, heat a small amount of oil in a skillet, add meat or vegetables and brown on medium-high heat. Turn meat or vegetables over and brown other side.

Or, place in broiler pan and lightly brush with oil, if desired. Broil 4 to 6 inches from source of heat until brown; turn and broil other side. Add to mixture in slow cooker and follow directions for the recipe.

Reducing Fat

- Purchase chops and roasts with thin layers of fat.

- Carefully trim all excess fat from meats before cooking.

- Add little or no oil or fat when cooking meats or sauces.

- After cooking and before serving, skim off excess fat.

- Cool any fatty cooked meat several hours or refrigerate overnight. Lift and discard solidified fat with spoon or spatula. Then reheat mixture on stovetop, in microwave or oven.

- Before adding fatty meat to slow cooker, quickly brown in a skillet or the oven. Discard drippings and follow directions for the recipe.

Food Safety Tips

- Wash hands and utensils between each step of food preparation.

- Use separate knives for cutting raw meat and vegetables.

- Don't thaw meat or poultry at room temperature. Thaw in the refrigerator or microwave, following manufacturer's directions.

- When serving, don't let cooked foods stand at room temperature more than two hours. Refrigerate leftovers promptly.

- Remember, keep hot foods hot and cold foods cold.

Less Than 6 Hours

Some new owners of slow cookers are surprised to learn there are few foods that can be slow cooked in less than 6 hours. Most main dishes with large pieces of meat require longer cooking time.

Chopped, thinly sliced, pounded or ground meats cook in less than 6 hours, unless they are combined with fibrous root vegetables. If you want to serve dinner within 6 hours, count on your slow cooker for *Apple Pork Curry, Turkey Sloppy Joes* or *Orange-Cranberry Chicken Breasts.*

Susie's Bean Dish

Makes 10 to 12 servings

This great dish for potluck suppers was created by Susie Lindquist, one of our contest winners.

1/2 lb. sliced bacon, chopped	3/4 cup packed brown sugar
1 lb. ground beef	1 (8-oz.) can tomato sauce
1/2 cup chopped onions	1 (20-oz.) can pork and beans
1 teaspoon salt	1 (15-oz.) can kidney beans, drained
1 teaspoon dry mustard	1 (15-oz.) can lima beans, drained
2 teaspoons cider vinegar	1 (15-oz.) can butter beans, drained
1/2 cup ketchup	

➤ In a skillet, cook bacon until limp but not crisp. Remove bacon and place in a slow cooker.

➤ Drain bacon drippings and brown ground beef in skillet until meat is no longer pink.

➤ Put beef and remaining ingredients in slow cooker, stir to combine. Cook on LOW 4-1/2 to 5 hours.

Each serving contains:

Cal	Prot	Carb	Fat	Chol	Sodium
369	22g	50g	10g	41mg	1143mg

Orange-Date Pudding

Makes 6 servings

Steaming in the slow cooker keeps this delicious favorite moist and tender. Pecans can be substituted for the dates.

3 eggs, separated

2-1/2 cups half-and-half

1/2 cup brown sugar

1/2 cup chopped dates

1/2 cup sweet orange marmalade

1/2 teaspoon almond extract

1/2 cup flaked coconut

2 cups stale French bread, cut in 1-inch cubes

1 teaspoon ground cinnamon

Whipped cream, garnish

➤ In a bowl, beat egg whites stiffly; set aside. In large bowl, beat egg yolks slightly and combine with half-and-half, sugar, dates, marmalade, almond extract, coconut and bread cubes. Thoroughly mix ingredients together. Fold in egg whites and sprinkle cinnamon on top.

➤ Place a trivet or metal rack in the bottom of a 4-quart or larger slow cooker. Pour in 1 to 2 cups hot water.

➤ Lightly butter a 2-quart bowl. Pour mixture into prepared bowl and cover with foil. Cover and cook on HIGH 2-1/2 hours.

➤ Pudding should be lightly puffed up, moist and browned around the edges. Remove and serve warm or cold.

Each serving contains:

Cal	Prot	Carb	Fat	Chol	Sodium
402	8g	53g	19g	154mg	169mg

Vegetable Turkey Round

Makes 5 or 6 servings

Cheesecloth holds mixture together while cooking and makes removal from pot easier. If you don't have cheesecloth, use a piece of white cotton cloth.

I medium potato, quartered, peeled	2 eggs, beaten slightly
I carrot, peeled	I teaspoon chopped fresh thyme
2 small zucchini, trimmed	I teaspoon chopped fresh sage
I small red bell pepper, chopped	I teaspoon Dijon-style mustard
I leek	1/2 teaspoon salt
1-1/2 lb. ground turkey	1/8 teaspoon pepper
I tablespoon tomato paste	I tablespoon Worcestershire sauce

➤ In food processor, shred potato, carrot and zucchini. Slice leek in half lengthwise, thoroughly rinse and cut into thin slices.

➤ Combine shredded potato, carrot, zucchini and red pepper with sliced leek, ground turkey, eggs, tomato paste and remaining ingredients. Shape into a 6-inch ball.

➤ Place rack in slow cooker. Place meat on a 9 by 24-inch double thickness of cheesecloth. Gently lift into pot on rack. Loosely fold cheesecloth over top of meat. Cover; cook on LOW 5-1/2 to 6 hours.

➤ Holding ends of cheesecloth, lift cooked meat from pot. Remove cheesecloth; cut meat into 5 or 6 wedges. Spoon drippings over wedges.

Each serving contains:

Cal	Prot	Carb	Fat	Chol	Sodium
279	26g	9g	15g	136mg	320mg

Apple Pork Curry

Makes 5 to 6 servings

An array of condiments lend texture, color and flavor. Curry enthusiasts may want to add more curry powder before thickening the mixture.

2 lb. lean pork, cut into 1/2-inch cubes

1 apple, chopped, peeled, cored

1 small onion, chopped

1 garlic clove, crushed

1 teaspoon instant chicken bouillon granules or 1 bouillon cube

1 tablespoon curry powder

1/8 teaspoon ground cinnamon

1/2 teaspoon ground ginger

1/2 teaspoon salt

1/2 cup orange juice

2 tablespoons cornstarch

2 tablespoons cold water

Cooked rice

Peanuts, chopped

Raisins

Coconut

Chutney

➤ In slow cooker, combine pork, apple, onion, garlic, bouillon, curry powder, cinnamon, ginger, salt and orange juice. Cover and cook on LOW 5 or 6 hours or until meat is tender.

➤ Turn pot on HIGH. In measuring cup, dissolve cornstarch in water. Stir into pork mixture. Cover and continue cooking on HIGH, stirring occasionally, 30 to 40 minutes or until thickened.

➤ Serve over cooked rice. Sprinkle with peanuts, raisins, coconut and chutney, if desired.

 Slices of fresh pineapple or melon topped with frozen yogurt make an ideal dessert after your curry dinner.

Each serving contains:

Cal	Prot	Carb	Fat	Chol	Sodium
278	32g	8g	12g	111mg	297mg

Pacific Rim Meatballs

Makes about 30 meatballs

Lowfat meatballs with a delicious oriental sweet-sour sauce.

1/4 cup low-salt soy sauce

2/3 cup orange juice

1/2 teaspoon grated orange peel

2 tablespoons hoisin sauce

1/4 cup dry white wine

2 tablespoons honey

1 tablespoon sesame oil

1 garlic clove, crushed

1-1/2 lb. chicken or turkey, skinned, boned, cubed

1/2 cup rolled oats

1 (8 oz.) can sliced water chestnuts, drained

1 egg

1/4 teaspoon salt

2 tablespoons cornstarch

2 tablespoons water

➤ In large bowl, combine soy sauce, orange juice and peel, hoisin sauce, wine, honey, oil and garlic; set aside.

➤ In food processor fitted with metal blade, process chicken or turkey until finely chopped. Add oats, water chestnuts, egg and salt. Process until water chestnuts are chopped.

➤ Form into 1-1/4- or 1-1/2-inch balls. Place in slow cooker. Add sauce mixture. Cover and cook on LOW 5-1/2 to 6 hours.

➤ With slotted spoon, remove meatballs; cover and keep warm. Turn pot on HIGH. Dissolve cornstarch in water. Add to sauce in pot; cook on HIGH, stirring occasionally, 20 to 30 minutes or until thickened. Serve over meatballs.

1 meatball contains:

Cal	Prot	Carb	Fat	Chol	Sodium
55	5g	5g	2g	20mg	128mg

Smoky Barbecue Ribs

Makes 6 servings

Balsamic vinegar lends a sublime flavor to this sauce.

2 tablespoons balsamic vinegar

1 tablespoon Dijon-style mustard

1 tablespoon Worcestershire sauce

2 tablespoons brown sugar

1 tablespoon soy sauce

1/4 teaspoon dried red pepper
   flakes, crumbled

1 teaspoon grated fresh ginger root

1/2 teaspoon liquid smoke

1 cup chili sauce

1/4 cup chopped green onions

4 lb. spareribs, cut into
   individual ribs

➤ In medium bowl, combine all ingredients except ribs. Dip each rib into sauce or brush sauce on both sides of ribs.

➤ Place coated ribs in slow cooker. Pour remaining sauce over ribs in pot. Cover and cook on LOW 5 to 6 hours or until meat is tender.

 Balsamic vinegar has a distinctive pungent flavor. If not available, use apple-cider vinegar.

Each serving contains:

Cal	Prot	Carb	Fat	Chol	Sodium
542	36g	17g	36g	143mg	948mg

Turkey Sloppy Joes

Makes 6 servings

A new version of the traditional Sloppy Joe. Great served on warm French rolls or whole-wheat hamburger buns.

1 red onion, chopped	1 garlic clove, crushed
1 yellow or green bell pepper, chopped	1 teaspoon Dijon-style mustard
1-1/2 lb. boneless turkey, finely chopped	1/4 teaspoon salt
	1/8 teaspoon pepper
1 cup bottled chili sauce or ketchup	6 French rolls

➤ Place onion, bell pepper and turkey in slow cooker.

➤ In small bowl, combine chili sauce or ketchup, garlic, mustard, salt and pepper. Pour over turkey-vegetable mixture; stir with fork to break up clusters of turkey. Cover and cook on LOW 4-1/2 to 6 hours or until turkey is very tender. Use a fork to break up any large chunks of turkey.

➤ Cut French rolls in half and toast. For each serving, spoon turkey mixture over 2 halves of open-face, toasted rolls.

Each serving contains:

Cal	Prot	Carb	Fat	Chol	Sodium
403	36g	48g	6g	66mg	1175mg

Mandarin-Style Pasta

Makes 6 servings

Make the sauce ahead of time, then reheat and add to cooked pasta at serving time.

1/2 cup hoisin sauce

3 tablespoons low-salt soy sauce

3/4 cup ketchup

1/4 cup dry sherry

1 garlic clove, crushed

2 teaspoons sesame oil

1/3 cup sliced green onion

1/8 teaspoon pepper

1-1/2 lb. uncooked turkey breast slices, cut into 1/4 by 1/2 by 1-inch strips

12 oz. angel hair (capellini) or fettuccine pasta, cooked

Toasted sesame seeds

➤ In large bowl, combine hoisin sauce, soy sauce, ketchup, sherry, garlic, sesame oil, green onion and pepper. Stir in turkey strips.

➤ Pour into slow cooker. Cover; cook on LOW 4-1/2 to 5 hours or until turkey is tender.

➤ Spoon over cooked pasta; toss. Sprinkle with sesame seeds.

 Hoisin sauce is a dark, spicy, sweetened soybean, chile pepper and garlic mixture.

Each serving contains:

Cal	Prot	Carb	Fat	Chol	Sodium
464	38g	60g	6g	66mg	1061mg

Sausage-Stuffed Chicken with Pine Nuts

Makes 6 servings

These unique flavor combinations complement each other.

6 chicken breast halves, boned, skinned

1/2 lb. Italian sausage

1 small onion, chopped

1/2 cup soft breadcrumbs

1/2 teaspoon grated lemon peel

1/4 cup pine nuts, chopped

1 tablespoon minced fresh parsley

1/2 teaspoon dried tarragon

1/4 teaspoon salt

1/8 teaspoon pepper

2 tablespoons dry white wine

Chopped parsley

➤ Place each chicken breast in small plastic bag or between sheets of waxed paper. Lightly pound with meat mallet; set aside.

➤ Remove casings from sausage. Crumble sausage into bowl; combine with onion, breadcrumbs, lemon peel, pine nuts, 1 tablespoon parsley, tarragon, salt and pepper. Form into 6 cylinders about 3-1/2 by 1-1/2 inches.

➤ Place one cylinder on center of each flattened chicken breast. Fold over and secure with small skewer.

➤ Place rack in bottom of slow cooker. Dip 24 by 14-inch cheesecloth into wine until moistened. Place on rack with ends extending up side of pot.

➤ Place chicken breasts on cheesecloth. Then fold cheesecloth ends over chicken. Cover and cook on LOW 4 hours or until chicken is tender.

➤ Holding the ends of cheesecloth, lift chicken from pot. Remove cheesecloth; sprinkle chicken with chopped parsley.

Each serving contains:

Cal	Prot	Carb	Fat	Chol	Sodium
301	34g	5g	16g	95mg	436mg

Orange-Cranberry Chicken Breasts

Makes 8 servings

A delicate orange sauce tops these stuffed chicken breasts.

1 cup chopped fresh cranberries

2 tablespoons brown sugar

5 slices cinnamon-raisin bread

2 tablespoons melted margarine or butter

1/4 teaspoon grated orange peel

8 chicken breast halves, boned, skinned

1/4 cup orange juice

2 tablespoons melted margarine or butter

1 orange, sliced

➤ In medium bowl, combine cranberries and brown sugar; set aside.

➤ Toast bread; cut into 1/2-inch cubes. Combine bread cubes, 2 tablespoons melted margarine or butter, orange peel and cranberry mixture.

➤ Place one chicken breast at a time in a small plastic bag or between sheets of waxed paper. Lightly pound with meat mallet. Repeat with all chicken breasts. Spoon about 1/3 cup cranberry mixture on center of each. Roll up; skewer to close.

➤ In shallow dish, combine orange juice and 2 tablespoons melted margarine or butter. Roll filled chicken breasts in orange-juice mixture. Place in slow cooker. Cover and cook on LOW about 5 hours.

➤ To serve, spoon drippings over chicken. Garnish with orange slices.

 When fresh cranberries are in season, buy several packages and freeze them for later use.

Each serving contains:

Cal	Prot	Carb	Fat	Chol	Sodium
252	28g	16g	8g	73mg	194mg

Stuffed Cabbage

Makes 9 or 10 rolls

Here is another version of the popular European favorite.

1 large head cabbage	1/8 teaspoon pepper
1 egg, beaten slightly	2 slices (about 2 oz.) boiled or baked ham, chopped
1 tablespoon chopped fresh parsley	2 cups (about 1 lb.) ground turkey
2 tablespoons chopped green onion	1 cup cooked rice
1 teaspoon chopped fresh sage	Bottled sweet-sour sauce, optional
1/2 teaspoon salt	

➤ Break off 9 or 10 large cabbage leaves. Drop into boiling water until limp. Drain and set aside.

➤ In medium bowl, combine egg, parsley, green onion, sage, salt, pepper, ham, turkey and rice.

➤ Spoon about 1/3 cup turkey mixture on each cabbage leaf. Fold in sides and roll ends over filling.

➤ Place seam-side down on rack in slow cooker. Cover; cook on LOW 5 to 6 hours.

➤ Serve plain or with bottled sweet-sour sauce, if desired.

 For easier rolling, trim thick base of each cabbage leaf before spooning on turkey mixture.

Each serving contains:

Cal	Prot	Carb	Fat	Chol	Sodium
133	12g	7g	6g	50mg	229mg

Fresh Artichokes

Makes 4 servings

Low-calorie artichokes are fun to eat! Dip tender ends of leaves and artichoke bottom into sauce or squeeze lemon juice over cooked artichoke.

2 large fresh artichokes
6 cups hot water
4 thin slices lemon

Lemon-Butter Sauce:
1/3 cup melted margarine or butter
3 tablespoons lemon juice
1/4 teaspoon seasoned salt

➤ With sharp knife, slice about 1 inch off top of each artichoke; cut off stem near base. With scissors, trim about 1/2 inch off top of each leaf. With sharp knife, halve each artichoke vertically, then scoop out and discard the fuzzy center or choke.

➤ Place artichoke halves in slow cooker; add hot water and lemon slices. Cover and cook on HIGH 4 to 5 hours or until done.

➤ Drain; serve with sauce.

Lemon-Butter Sauce: Combine melted margarine or butter, lemon juice and seasoned salt.

 The artichoke is an edible bud of the cynara scolymus *thistle.*

Each serving with sauce contains:

Cal	Prot	Carb	Fat	Chol	Sodium
156	4g	12g	12g	0mg	380mg

Yankee Yams

Makes about 6 servings

This yummy yam dish enjoys a nice flavor contrast with the slightly tart apples accented by maple syrup.

2 tablespoons softened margarine
  or butter

5 medium yams or sweet potatoes

3 cooking apples, peeled, cored,
  cut into 8 wedges

1/4 teaspoon ground nutmeg

1/4 cup maple-flavored syrup

2 tablespoons melted margarine
  or butter

2 tablespoons chopped pecans,
  optional

➤ Brush 2 tablespoons softened margarine or butter on bottom and about 6 inches up sides of slow cooker.

➤ Peel yams or sweet potatoes; cut crosswise into 1/2-inch slices. Place on bottom of slow cooker. Top with apple wedges; then nutmeg, maple syrup and 2 tablespoons melted margarine or butter.

➤ Cover and cook on LOW 3-1/2 to 4 hours or until tender.

➤ Sprinkle with pecans, if desired.

Each serving contains:

Cal	Prot	Carb	Fat	Chol	Sodium
219	2g	41g	6g	0mg	105mg

Salsa-Topped Onions

Makes 6 servings

This interesting recipe can perk up a menu of bland foods. Try serving with broiled chicken or fish.

3 medium onions, peeled, halved crosswise

2 tablespoons chopped cilantro

1 jalapeño pepper, seeded, chopped

2 small tomatoes, peeled, seeded, chopped

1 garlic clove, crushed

1 tablespoon red-wine vinegar

2 tablespoons vegetable oil

1/4 teaspoon salt

➤ Place onion halves cut-side up in slow cooker.

➤ In small bowl, combine cilantro, jalapeño, tomatoes, garlic, vinegar, oil and salt. Spoon over onions. If all onions do not fit in one layer, place 3 halves on bottom and top with half the sauce.

➤ Lightly cover with heavy-duty foil. Arrange remaining halves and sauce on top. Cover and cook on LOW 5 to 6 hours or until onions are tender. Serve warm or cold.

 Cilantro, a member of the parsley family, is also known as coriander or Chinese parsley.

Each serving contains:

Cal	Prot	Carb	Fat	Chol	Sodium
58	1g	4g	5g	0mg	115mg

Fresh Tomato Soup

Makes 6 servings

Italian or plum tomatoes are ideal for this dish, but regular tomatoes may be used.

8 medium tomatoes

1 medium onion, chopped

2 carrots, peeled, thinly sliced

1 garlic clove, crushed

1 tablespoon brown sugar

1 tablespoon chopped fresh basil

1 tablespoon chopped parsley

2 teaspoons Worcestershire sauce

1/2 teaspoon salt

1/8 teaspoon pepper

3 cups chicken broth or bouillon

➤ Drop tomatoes in a pan of boiling water for 15 to 20 seconds; immediately rinse with cold water. Remove skins. Cut in half crosswise; squeeze out and discard seeds.

➤ Combine tomatoes in slow cooker with onions, carrots, garlic, brown sugar, basil, parsley, Worcestershire sauce, salt, pepper and broth or bouillon. Cover and cook on LOW 5 to 6 hours or until vegetables are very soft.

➤ Purée in blender or food processor fitted with metal blade. Serve in individual bowls.

Each serving contains:

Cal	Prot	Carb	Fat	Chol	Sodium
79	4g	14g	1g	1mg	279mg

Potato & Leek Chowder

Makes 5 or 6 servings

Using nonfat dry milk powder gives the appearance and taste of milk without the fat and calorie count of whole milk.

3 medium potatoes, peeled, diced

1 (11-oz.) can whole-kernel corn, not drained

1/2 cup chopped celery

1 (1.8-oz.) pkg. leek soup mix

4 cups water

1 cup nonfat dry milk powder

1/2 cup (2 oz.) shredded Jarlsberg or Swiss cheese, optional

➤ In slow cooker, combine potatoes, corn, celery, dry leek soup mix and water. Cover and cook on LOW 5 to 6 hours or until potatoes and celery are tender.

➤ Just before serving, gradually add dry milk powder to hot soup; gently whisk until well blended.

➤ Ladle into individual bowls; sprinkle with cheese, if desired.

 *Jarlsberg is a mild-flavored Norwegian cheese.*

Each serving contains:

Cal	Prot	Carb	Fat	Chol	Sodium
176	8g	35g	2g	3mg	631mg

Caramel-Apple Euphoria

Makes 7 servings

Treat yourself to this people-pleasing dessert. Try substituting ripe peaches for apples and 1/8 teaspoon almond extract for cardamom.

2 medium (5 to 6 oz. each) cooking apples

1/2 cup apple juice

24 (about 7 oz.) caramel candy squares, unwrapped

1 teaspoon vanilla extract

1/8 teaspoon ground cardamom

1/2 teaspoon ground cinnamon

1/3 cup cream-style peanut butter

7 slices angel-food cake or 1 quart vanilla ice cream

➤ Peel, core and cut each apple into 18 wedges; set aside.

➤ In 3-1/2 quart or smaller slow cooker, combine apple juice, unwrapped caramel candies, vanilla, cardamom and cinnamon.

➤ Drop peanut butter, 1 teaspoon at a time, over ingredients in slow cooker; stir.

➤ Add apple wedges; cover and cook on LOW 5 hours.

➤ Stir contents of slow cooker thoroughly; cover and cook on LOW 1 additional hour.

➤ Serve approximately 1/3 cup of warm caramel-apple mixture over a slice of angel-food cake or vanilla ice cream.

1 serving sauce contains:

Cal	Prot	Carb	Fat	Chol	Sodium
216	4g	32g	9g	1mg	67mg

1 serving with cake contains:

Cal	Prot	Carb	Fat	Chol	Sodium
341	7g	61g	9g	1mg	336mg

1 serving with ice cream contains:

Cal	Prot	Carb	Fat	Chol	Sodium
369	7g	50g	17g	35mg	133mg

Sweet Potato Pudding

Makes 5 or 6 servings

If you're feasting Hawaiian-style, this is the perfect dessert to serve afterward.

3 large sweet potatoes, cooked, peeled, cubed

1/2 cup brown sugar

3/4 cup milk

2 eggs

1/2 teaspoon ground allspice

1/2 teaspoon ground cinnamon

1/2 teaspoon grated orange peel

1 tablespoon softened margarine or butter

Whipped cream

Chopped macadamia nuts or pecans

➤ In food processor fitted with metal blade, combine cooked sweet potatoes, brown sugar, milk, eggs, allspice, cinnamon and orange peel. Process until smooth.

➤ Grease bottom and sides of slow cooker with margarine or butter. Spoon in potato mixture. Cover and cook on HIGH 2 to 3 hours or until mixture is puffed, firm and edges begin to brown.

➤ Serve warm or cold. Top each serving with a dab of whipped cream and chopped nuts.

Each serving contains:

Cal	Prot	Carb	Fat	Chol	Sodium
181	4g	34g	4g	74mg	73mg

Albóndigas

Makes 8 servings

Garnish this popular Mexican soup with sprigs of fresh cilantro or mint, and serve with warm flour tortillas.

1/2 lb. ground beef
1/2 onion, minced
2 garlic cloves, minced
1/4 cup uncooked instant rice
1 egg
Salt and pepper, to taste
1 (4-oz.) can roasted green chiles, drained, chopped

1 carrot, shredded
1 (14-1/2-oz.) can stewed tomatoes
4 cups hot water
2 cups beef broth or water
1 teaspoon dried oregano leaves
2 tablespoons chopped fresh parsley or cilantro

➤ In a bowl, combine beef, onion, garlic, rice, egg, salt and pepper to taste. Form into 1-1/2-inch meatballs.

➤ Place chiles and shredded carrot in bottom of slow cooker. Spoon tomatoes evenly on top. Place meatballs on top of tomatoes.

➤ Pour in water, broth, oregano and parsley or cilantro.

➤ Cover and cook on LOW 5-1/2 to 6 hours.

Each serving contains:

Cal	Prot	Carb	Fat	Chol	Sodium
106	8g	9g	4g	46mg	441mg

6 to 8 Hours

A vast variety of dishes are ready within 6 to 8 hours. It's possible to make *Pizza Soup* with all the popular pizza flavors, including sausage, tomatoes, peppers, mushrooms and shredded mozzarella as a topping. Or, make *Chinese Braised Chicken* with oriental overtones. For meat dishes, *Spaghetti 'n' Meatballs* or *Beef 'n' Turkey Sausage Chili* will cook in under 8 hours. There's also time to cook *Orange Chutney Steak* in a spicy beer sauce.

Chinese Braised Chicken

Makes about 5 servings

Congratulations to Janet Hill, first-place winner of our Crockery Favorites contest.

1 cup chopped onions

1 (3-lb.) chicken, whole or cut up

1 cup water

1/2 cup lite soy sauce

2 tablespoons chopped
fresh ginger

2 tablespoons sugar

1 garlic clove, crushed

Salt and pepper, to taste

Chinese Relish

1 cup finely chopped green onions

1/3 cup chopped fresh cilantro

1 tablespoon grated fresh ginger

1/2 teaspoon sesame oil

1 tablespoon rice-wine vinegar
or sherry

Salt and pepper, to taste

Toasted sesame seeds, for garnish

➤ Place onions in a slow cooker; add chicken. If using whole chicken, place breast side down.

➤ In a small bowl combine water, soy sauce, ginger, sugar and garlic; pour over chicken. Cover and cook on LOW 6 to 7 hours. Season with salt and pepper, to taste.

➤ Serve with Chinese Relish, recipe follows, and top with sesame seeds.

Chinese Relish: In a small serving bowl combine all ingredients. Season with salt and pepper, to taste.

Each serving contains:

Cal	Prot	Carb	Fat	Chol	Sodium
664	54g	14g	43g	204mg	1113mg

Chinese Braised Chicken, page 22

Beef 'n' Turkey-Sausage Chili, page 33

Continental Steak Round-up

Makes 6 to 8 servings

Hazelnuts and apricots combined with bok choy create a surprisingly delicious filling.

1-1/2 to 2 lb. boneless beef round steak
1/4 teaspoon salt
1/8 teaspoon black pepper
1 medium head bok choy
1/4 cup toasted, chopped hazelnuts

1/3 cup chopped dried apricots
3/4 cup soft bread crumbs
1/4 teaspoon ground allspice
1/4 cup red wine
4 teaspoons cornstarch
2 tablespoons cold water

➤ Trim excess fat from round steak. Pound steak to 1/2 inch thickness. Sprinkle with salt and pepper.

➤ Remove large outer leaves of bok choy and set aside. Thinly slice smaller leaves crosswise to make 1 cup.

➤ In a medium bowl combine bok choy, hazelnuts, apricots, breadcrumbs and allspice. Spread evenly over steak; roll up starting at short end. Place seam side down in slow cooker. Pour wine over meat.

➤ Separate leaves from stalks of reserved bok choy. Place stalks in bottom of pot, around meat. Cover meat with large leaves. Cover pot and cook on LOW 6 to 7 hours.

➤ Remove meat and bok choy; keep warm. Turn control to HIGH. Dissolve cornstarch in water and stir into juice in pot. Cover and cook on high about 15 minutes or until slightly thickened. Slice neatly crosswise and serve with gravy.

Each serving contains:

Cal	Prot	Carb	Fat	Chol	Sodium
349	32g	10g	19g	81mg	200mg

Cranberry Chicken

Makes 8 servings

Serve over wide egg noodles or rice and garnish with Mandarin orange segments.

1/4 cup oil

2 broiler-fryers, quartered

1 cup chopped onion

1 tablespoon grated orange peel

1/2 cup orange juice concentrate

1 tablespoon lemon juice

1 (16-oz.) can whole cranberry sauce

1-1/2 teaspoons ground cinnamon

1 teaspoon ground ginger

1/2 teaspoon salt

2 tablespoons cornstarch or all-purpose flour

1/4 cup water

➤ Heat oil in a large skillet and add chicken pieces. Place onions in a 5-quart slow cooker. Place chicken on top.

➤ In a bowl, combine remaining ingredients, except cornstarch and water, and pour over chicken. Cover and cook on LOW about 6 hours.

➤ Remove chicken and cover. Turn slow cooker to HIGH. Blend together cornstarch and water, stir into juices until slightly thickened. Serve over chicken.

Each serving contains:

Cal	Prot	Carb	Fat	Chol	Sodium
192	1g	33g	7g	0mg	151mg

Vegetarian Split-Pea Soup

Makes 8 servings

Herbs supply extra flavor to an old favorite.

1 lb. dried split peas	2 bay leaves
1 leek, rinsed, chopped	1/4 cup chopped parsley
2 celery ribs, chopped	1 teaspoon dried oregano leaves
1 potato, peeled, chopped	Salt and pepper, to taste
1/2 teaspoon crushed garlic	Chopped parsley for garnish
7 cups hot water	

➤ In a slow cooker, combine all ingredients. Cover and cook on LOW 7 to 8 hours. Remove bay leaves at end of cooking time.

➤ If you like a smoother consistency, purée in a blender or food processor fitted with a metal blade.

➤ Serve soup in individual bowls. Garnish with chopped parsley.

 For faster preparation, chop the leek, celery and carrots in a food processor.

Each serving contains:

Cal	Prot	Carb	Fat	Chol	Sodium
232	15g	43g	1g	0mg	64mg

Spaghetti 'n' Meatballs

Makes 6 to 7 servings

Everybody's favorite—a good, old-fashioned spaghetti dinner.

I onion, chopped

I carrot, peeled, chopped

I stalk celery, chopped

I garlic clove, crushed

I (8-oz.) can tomato sauce

1/4 cup dry red wine

2 teaspoons chopped fresh basil

2 teaspoons chopped fresh oregano

I teaspoon chopped fresh thyme

I teaspoon Worcestershire sauce

1/2 teaspoon salt

1/8 teaspoon pepper

I (28-oz.) can Italian tomatoes with juice

I lb. lean ground beef

1/2 lb. mild Italian sausage

1/2 cup seasoned dry breadcrumbs

I egg, beaten slightly

1/4 cup milk

I lb. spaghetti, cooked

Grated Parmesan cheese, optional

➤ In slow cooker, combine onion, carrot, celery, garlic, tomato sauce, wine, basil, oregano, thyme, Worcestershire sauce, salt and pepper. Chop tomatoes and add to mixture in slow cooker.

➤ In medium bowl, combine beef, sausage, breadcrumbs, egg and milk. Form into 20 to 22 (1-1/2-inch) meatballs. Carefully place in sauce in slow cooker. Cover and cook on LOW 7 to 8 hours.

➤ Spoon hot mixture over cooked spaghetti or other pasta. Sprinkle with grated Parmesan cheese, if desired.

Each serving contains:

Cal	Prot	Carb	Fat	Chol	Sodium
483	26g	57g	16g	85mg	847mg

Turkey Ranchero

Makes 8 servings

For variety, omit corn chips and serve turkey over cooked rice or noodles. Delicious also as a filling for tacos or tostadas. Use either corn or flour tortillas.

4 turkey thighs (4-1/2 to 5 lb.)

1 (1-5/8-oz.) pkg. enchilada sauce mix

1 (6-oz.) can tomato paste

1/4 cup water

1 cup (4 oz.) grated Monterey Jack cheese

1/3 cup lowfat yogurt or dairy sour cream

1/4 cup sliced green onions

1/2 cup sliced ripe olives

1-1/2 cups corn chips, crushed

➤ With sharp knife, cut each thigh in half; remove bone and skin. Place in slow cooker.

➤ Combine dry enchilada sauce mix with tomato paste and water. Mixture will be thick. Spread over turkey thighs. Cover; cook on LOW 7 to 8 hours or until tender.

➤ Turn pot on HIGH. Add cheese; stir until cheese melts. Spoon into an au gratin dish or shallow casserole. Spoon yogurt or sour cream over turkey. Sprinkle with green onions and olives. Top with corn chips.

Each serving contains:

Cal	Prot	Carb	Fat	Chol	Sodium
383	42g	11g	18g	121mg	346mg

Orange Chutney Steak

Makes 6 to 7 servings

This is ideal for the larger slow cooker. Edges of the meat will extend an inch or two up the sides of 3-1/2-quart pot.

1 (1-1/2 lb.) flank steak

2 cups mixed dried fruits

2 tablespoons orange marmalade

2 tablespoons brown sugar

2 tablespoons lemon juice

1/4 teaspoon ground ginger

1/4 teaspoon ground cinnamon

1 teaspoon Worcestershire® sauce

1/4 teaspoon salt

1/8 teaspoon pepper

1 (12-oz.) can beer

2 tablespoons cornstarch

2 tablespoons cold water

Cooked rice

➤ Place whole flank steak in slow cooker.

➤ In medium bowl, combine dried fruits, marmalade, brown sugar, lemon juice, ginger, cinnamon, Worcestershire sauce, salt, pepper and beer. Pour over meat. Cover and cook on LOW about 7 hours.

➤ With slotted spoon, remove meat and fruit; keep warm. Turn pot on HIGH. In small bowl, dissolve cornstarch in cold water. Stir into juices in pot. Cover and cook on HIGH 15 to 20 minutes or until thickened, stirring occasionally.

➤ Spoon over warm meat and fruit. Serve on a bed of rice.

 Apple juice can be substituted for the beer.

Each serving contains:

Cal	Prot	Carb	Fat	Chol	Sodium
266	21g	27g	7g	49mg	164mg

Sun-dried Tomato Meat Loaf

Makes 6 or 7 wedges

Italian flavors dominate in this special dish.

1-1/2 lb. lean ground beef	1/2 cup milk
1/2 lb. Italian sausage	1/2 teaspoon salt
1 small onion, chopped	1/2 teaspoon dried Italian seasoning
1 cup instant potato flakes not reconstituted (dry)	3 tablespoons chopped sun-dried tomatoes
1 egg, beaten slightly	1 celery stalk, chopped
1 cup beef broth or bouillon	

➤ In large bowl, combine all ingredients. Shape into a 7-inch ball.

➤ Place a trivet in slow cooker. Place meatball on double thickness of cheese-cloth (about 24 inches square). Holding ends of cheesecloth, gently lower meat into pot. Loosely fold cheesecloth over top of meat. Cover; cook on LOW 6 to 7 hours.

➤ Holding ends of cheesecloth, lift meat from pot. Cut into wedges.

Each wedge contains:

Cal	Prot	Carb	Fat	Chol	Sodium
287	22g	7g	19g	103mg	444mg

Mexican-Style Pizza

Makes 6 or 8 servings

Try using other combinations of toppings, such as fresh pork sausage, anchovies, olives, Canadian bacon or green peppers.

2 (8-oz.) cans tomato sauce

2 garlic cloves

2 teaspoons dried oregano leaves

2 teaspoons dried basil leaves

1/2 teaspoon celery salt

1/4 teaspoon salt

1/8 teaspoon pepper

5 (6-inch) corn tortillas

5 teaspoons grated Parmesan cheese

1 medium onion, thinly sliced, separated into rings

2 large plum tomatoes, thinly sliced

1-1/2 oz. thinly sliced pepperoni

2 tablespoons chopped parsley

8 oz. mozzarella cheese, sliced

➤ In blender or food processor fitted with metal blade, combine tomato sauce, garlic, oregano, basil, celery salt, salt and pepper. Process 3 minutes or until puréed; set aside.

➤ Spread each tortilla with about 2-1/2 tablespoons tomato purée; sprinkle each with 1 teaspoon grated Parmesan cheese. On each tortilla, spread about 1/5 of the following: onion rings, tomato slices, pepperoni, parsley and mozzarella cheese.

➤ Place each prepared tortilla in slow cooker, one on top of the other. Pour any remaining tomato purée over stacked tortillas in slow cooker. Cover; cook on LOW 7 to 8 hours.

➤ Spoon pizza into a serving bowl. Or, with long-bladed knife, cut pizza into 6 or 8 wedges and remove wedges to a serving platter with a metal spatula. Spoon any sauce remaining in the slow cooker over pizza in bowl or on platter.

Each serving contains:

Cal	Prot	Carb	Fat	Chol	Sodium
181	12g	16g	8g	18mg	825mg

Smoked Sausage with Red Cabbage & Sweet Potatoes

Makes 5 or 6 servings

This German-inspired dish is designed to convert the most reluctant vegetable eater. It combines both spicy and sweet flavors. Serve with pumpernickel bread.

1 small head red cabbage, thinly sliced

2 medium sweet potatoes, peeled, cut into 1/2-inch slices

1 cooking apple, peeled, cored, thinly sliced

1 lb. smoked sausage ring, cut into 1-inch slices

2 tablespoons brown sugar

1/8 teaspoon ground cinnamon

1/4 cup red-wine vinegar

Dijon-style or sweet-hot mustard

➤ In the slow cooker, make alternate layers of cabbage, sweet potatoes, apple and sausage.

➤ In small bowl, combine brown sugar, cinnamon and vinegar. Pour over ingredients in pot. Cover and cook on LOW 7 to 8 hours. Serve with mustard.

Each serving contains:

Cal	Prot	Carb	Fat	Chol	Sodium
340	12g	22g	23g	53mg	727mg

Lamb 'n' Lentil Stew

Makes about 8 servings

Satisfy those hearty appetites with this stick-to-the-ribs dish. Hot biscuits and a salad complete your meal.

1 lb. lean lamb shoulder, cut into 1-inch cubes

1 garlic clove, crushed

1 lb. zucchini, cut crosswise into 1/2-inch slices

1 medium tomato, peeled, seeded, diced

1 teaspoon chopped fresh rosemary leaves

2 teaspoons balsamic vinegar

1/2 teaspoon salt

1/8 teaspoon pepper

1 cup dried lentils

3 cups beef broth or bouillon

2 cups water

Chopped fresh cilantro

In slow cooker, combine all ingredients except cilantro. Cover and cook on LOW 7 to 8 hours or until lentils are tender. Sprinkle with cilantro.

 Make a complete one-dish meal by adding Baked Cheddar Topping, page 118.

Each serving contains:

Cal	Prot	Carb	Fat	Chol	Sodium
203	22g	15g	7g	52mg	170mg

Beef 'n' Turkey–Sausage Chili

Makes 5 or 6 servings

Perhaps this sounds like an unusual combination of meats, but you might like it more than traditional chili.

1-1/2 lb. boneless beef chuck, diced

1/2 lb. turkey sausage

1 red or yellow bell pepper, seeded, chopped

1 onion, chopped

1 garlic clove, crushed

1 (6-oz.) can tomato paste

1 (12-oz.) can beer

1 teaspoon instant beef boullion granules

1 jalapeño pepper, seeded, minced

2 teaspoons chili powder

1 teaspoon ground cumin

1/4 teaspoon salt

1/2 cup plain lowfat yogurt or dairy sour cream

2 tablespoons chopped fresh cilantro

1/4 cup chopped green onions

➤ In slow cooker, combine all ingredients except garnishes. Cover and cook on LOW 7 to 8 hours or until beef is tender.

➤ Spoon into individual bowls. Top with yogurt or sour cream, cilantro and green onions.

Each serving contains:

Cal	Prot	Carb	Fat	Chol	Sodium
377	35g	12g	19g	117mg	676mg

Lamb Curry

Makes 5 to 6 servings

Turn this recipe into party fare with lively condiments of chutney, chopped peanuts, raisins, shredded coconut, mandarin orange segments and chopped green onions.

1/2 cup chopped, dried figs	1/4 teaspoon ground mace
1 onion, chopped	1/2 teaspoon ground coriander
2 stalks celery, finely chopped	1/2 teaspoon salt
1 garlic clove, crushed	1 cup chicken broth or bouillon
1-1/4 to 1-1/2 lb. boneless lamb stew meat, cut into 1-inch cubes	1 tablespoon cornstarch
	1 tablespoon cold water
1 tablespoon curry powder	Cooked rice

➤ In slow cooker, combine figs, onion, celery and garlic. Add lamb, curry powder, mace, coriander, salt and broth or bouillon. Cover and cook on LOW 7 to 8 hours.

➤ Turn pot on HIGH. Dissolve cornstarch in water. Stir into cooked curry. Cover and cook on HIGH 15 or 20 minutes, stirring occasionally. Serve over cooked rice.

Each serving contains:

Cal	Prot	Carb	Fat	Chol	Sodium
155	21g	3g	6g	64mg	239mg

Smoky Kidney Beans

Makes about 8 cups

Because of their dense texture, kidney beans are at their best when cooked on HIGH.

1 lb. dried kidney beans, rinsed

6 cups water

1 medium onion, chopped

1/2 lb. smoked sausage (keilbasa), diced

1/4 cup brown sugar, lightly packed

2 tablespoons Dijon-style mustard

1 teaspoon Worcestershire sauce

1 garlic clove, crushed

1/3 cup molasses

1/3 cup ketchup

1/8 teaspoon ground cloves

1/2 teaspoon salt

1/8 teaspoon pepper

➤ In slow cooker, combine dried beans and water; let stand overnight or at least 8 hours. Drain; reserve 2-1/2 cups liquid from beans.

➤ In slow cooker, combine drained beans, remaining ingredients and reserved 2-1/2 cups of liquid. Cover and cook on HIGH about 7 hours or until beans are tender.

1 cup contains:

Cal	Prot	Carb	Fat	Chol	Sodium
303	14g	44g	9g	19mg	621mg

Red Cabbage & Apples

Makes about 6 cups

This classic German side dish is traditionally served with venison.

1 small head red cabbage,
  thinly sliced

2 apples, seeded, chopped

1 medium onion, chopped

1 tablespoon brown sugar

1/4 teaspoon salt

1/8 teaspoon pepper

1/8 teaspoon ground mace

1/4 cup dry red wine

1/2 cup apple juice

➤ Combine cabbage, apples, onion, brown sugar, salt, pepper and mace in slow cooker. Pour wine and apple juice over all. Cover and cook on LOW 6-1/2 to 7 hours.

➤ Serve as an accompaniment to pork roast or chops.

 If you're using a 3-1/2-quart slow cooker, be sure to use a small head of cabbage, because a large amount of cabbage will not fit.

1 cup contains:

Cal	Prot	Carb	Fat	Chol	Sodium
68	1g	15g	0g	0mg	98mg

Gingery Tomato Soup

Makes 5 servings

A hint of ginger makes this light soup an interesting first course for dinner.

1 (14-1/2-oz.) can Italian-style
   tomatoes, coarsely chopped,
   not drained

1 (6-oz.) can tomato paste

1 garlic clove, crushed

1 red or yellow bell pepper, seeded,
   chopped

1 tablespoon chopped, crystallized
   ginger

1 teaspoon grated orange peel

1/2 cup orange juice

1/8 teaspoon ground ginger

2 cups chicken broth or bouillon

1 tablespoon brown sugar

1/4 teaspoon salt

1/8 teaspoon pepper

1 orange, cut in thin slices

➤ In slow cooker, combine all ingredients except orange slices.
Cover and cook on LOW 7 to 8 hours.

➤ Purée in blender or food processor fitted with metal blade.

➤ Serve in individual bowls. Garnish each with orange slice.

 *Orange and tomato flavors enhance one another. Try this and see for
yourself what a treat it is.*

Each serving contains:

Cal	Prot	Carb	Fat	Chol	Sodium
98	5g	20g	1g	0mg	264mg

Pizza Soup

Makes 6 to 7 servings

Unmistakable flavors in a different form. Serve with garlic bread and a mixed green salad.

2 (14-oz.) cans Italian-style sliced
   tomatoes

2 cups beef broth or bouillon

1 onion, sliced

1 small red or green bell pepper,
   seeded, sliced

1 cup sliced mushrooms

1/2 lb. smoked sausage links,
   thinly sliced

1 teaspoon chopped fresh oregano

1 cup (4 oz.) shredded mozzarella
   or Cheddar cheese

➤ In slow cooker, combine tomatoes, broth or bouillon, onion, pepper, mushrooms, sausage and oregano. Cover and cook on LOW 7 to 8 hours.

➤ Spoon into individual bowls. Top with cheese.

Each serving contains:

Cal	Prot	Carb	Fat	Chol	Sodium
188	11g	7g	13g	32mg	576mg

Hot 'n' Sour Soup

Makes 7 to 8 servings

We thank the Chinese for a light, pleasingly spicy soup with stick-to-the-ribs ingredients.

1/2 lb. lean pork, cut into thin strips

1/4 lb. (about 7) fresh mushrooms, sliced

1 (8-oz.) can sliced water chestnuts, drained

1/2 cup bamboo shoots, cut into strips

2 tablespoons rice-wine vinegar

2 tablespoons soy sauce

1 teaspoon sesame oil

1/4 teaspoon dried red-pepper flakes

1 cup cubed firm tofu, cut into 1/2-inch cubes

2 cups chicken broth or bouillon

2 cups water

Green onion slices for garnish

➤ In slow cooker, combine all ingredients except green onions. Cover; cook on LOW 7 to 8 hours.

➤ Ladle into individual bowls. Garnish with green-onion slices.

 Bamboo shoots can be found canned in the Asian food section of your market.

Each serving contains:

Cal	Prot	Carb	Fat	Chol	Sodium
108	11g	6g	5g	22mg	282mg

Country-Style Chicken Soup

Makes 8 or 9 servings

An abundant amount of chicken makes this a hearty main dish.

1 (3- to 4-lb.) chicken, cut up	1 bay leaf
1 onion or leek, chopped	1 teaspoon chopped fresh thyme
1 carrot, finely chopped	1/2 teaspoon salt
1/2 cup chopped celery	1/8 teaspoon pepper
2 tablespoons chopped fresh parsley	6 cups water
	4 oz. cooked fine egg noodles or 3 cups cooked rice

➤ In 4-quart or larger slow cooker, combine chicken, onion or leek, carrot, celery, parsley, bay leaf, thyme, salt, pepper and water. Cover and cook on LOW 7 or 8 hours or until tender.

➤ Remove chicken and bay leaf. Turn cooker on HIGH. Remove meat from chicken parts; cut into bite-size pieces.

➤ Return chicken to slow cooker; add cooked noodles or rice. Serve when heated to desired temperature.

Each serving contains:

Cal	Prot	Carb	Fat	Chol	Sodium
188	23g	10g	6g	74mg	183mg

Potato Leek Soup

Makes about 8 servings

A popular year-round soup featuring potatoes and leeks, accented with sour cream.

3 medium potatoes, peeled, chopped

1 carrot, peeled, finely chopped

2 leeks, washed, sliced crosswise

1 teaspoon chopped fresh thyme

1/4 teaspoon salt

1/8 teaspoon pepper

4 cups chicken broth or bouillon

1 cup dairy sour cream

Ground nutmeg

➤ In slow cooker, combine potatoes, carrot, leeks, thyme, salt, pepper and broth or bouillon. Cover and cook on LOW 6 or 7 hours or until potatoes are soft. Stir in sour cream.

➤ Spoon into soup bowls; sprinkle with nutmeg.

 Although leeks look like they would have a strong flavor, their flavor is very mild.

Each serving contains:

Cal	Prot	Carb	Fat	Chol	Sodium
147	5g	17g	7g	13mg	93mg

Green Chile Chowder

Makes 8 servings

A colorful chowder, ideal for chilly weather.

1 (15- or 16-1/2-oz.) can
    cream-style corn

2 potatoes, peeled, diced

2 tablespoons chopped fresh chives

1 (4-oz.) can diced green chiles,
    drained

1 (2-oz.) jar pimientos, chopped

1/2 cup chopped ham

3 cups chicken broth or bouillon

1 cup milk or light cream

1 cup (4 oz.) shredded Monterey
    Jack cheese

➤ In slow cooker, combine corn, potatoes, chives, chiles, pimientos, ham and broth or bouillon. Cover and cook on LOW 7 to 8 hours or until potatoes are tender.

➤ Stir in milk or light cream. Reheat, if desired.

➤ Serve in individual bowls; sprinkle with shredded cheese.

Each serving contains:

Cal	Prot	Carb	Fat	Chol	Sodium
170	10g	20g	6g	20mg	507mg

Pork 'n' Noodle Soup

Makes 6 to 7 servings

Cellophane noodles add extra interest to this unusual soup.

1/2 lb. lean pork, cut into 1/2-inch cubes

2 medium turnips, peeled, cut into 1/4 by 2-inch strips

1 medium carrot, peeled, thinly sliced crosswise

3 green onions, cut into 1/2-inch pieces

2 teaspoons soy sauce

2 tablespoons sherry

1/8 teaspoon pepper

4 cups chicken broth or bouillon

2 oz. cellophane noodles, broken into 3- or 4-inch lengths

➤ In slow cooker, combine all ingredients except noodles. Cover and cook on LOW 6 to 7 hours.

➤ About 15 minutes before serving, place noodles in a large saucepan or heat-proof bowl; cover with boiling water. Let stand 10 minutes. Drain; add to mixture in slow cooker. Ladle into individual bowls.

 Cellophane or transparent noodles are widely used in both Chinese and Japanese cuisines. In India, they are called China Grass.

Each serving contains:

Cal	Prot	Carb	Fat	Chol	Sodium
99	10g	5g	4g	25mg	140mg

Garden Gate Soup

Makes about 6 servings

Apples team up with vegetables for this golden, smooth, mouth-watering soup.

1 to 1-1/2 lb. banana squash, peeled, seeded, cubed

1 cooking apple, peeled, cubed

1 large sweet potato, peeled, cubed

1 small onion, sliced

1 teaspoon curry powder

2 teaspoons Worcestershire sauce

3 cups apple juice

1/4 teaspoon salt

1/3 cup dairy sour cream or plain yogurt, stirred

Ground nutmeg

➤ In slow cooker, combine squash, apple, potato, onion, curry powder, Worcestershire sauce, apple juice and salt. Cover and cook on LOW 6 to 7 hours or until vegetables are tender.

➤ Purée half at a time, in blender or food processor fitted with metal blade.

➤ Stir in sour cream or yogurt. Sprinkle with nutmeg.

Each serving contains:

Cal	Prot	Carb	Fat	Chol	Sodium
160	3g	32g	3g	6mg	123mg

Piña Colada Bread Pudding

Makes 8 or 10 servings

This dessert is also delicious cold. Spoon into serving dish, cover and refrigerate; eat later.

1 (1-lb.) unsliced loaf French or sourdough bread

1 (10-oz.) can frozen Piña Colada drink mix

1 (6-oz.) can pineapple juice

1 (12-oz.) can evaporated skimmed milk

1/2 cup cream of coconut

2 (7 or 8 oz. each) ripe bananas, sliced crosswise

3 eggs

1/3 cup Irish cream or 1/4 cup light rum, optional

1 cup golden raisins

1 (8-oz.) can crushed pineapple and juice

1 teaspoon grated lemon peel

8 or 10 fresh mint sprigs

➤ With sharp knife, trim crust from bread; discard crust or make into breadcrumbs for use in another recipe. Cut bread into 1-inch cubes; set aside.

➤ In blender or food processor fitted with metal blade, combine half of the following ingredients: drink mix, pineapple juice, milk, cream of coconut and banana slices. Process until puréed; pour purée into 6-cup bowl.

➤ Purée remaining half of liquid ingredients and banana slices as well as eggs and liqueur, if desired. Combine both purées. Combine raisins and crushed pineapple with juice; set aside.

➤ Place about 2/3 of bread cubes in slow cooker; sprinkle 1/2 teaspoon grated lemon peel and spread 1 cup raisin-pineapple mixture over bread in slow cooker. Top with remaining bread cubes; then with remaining lemon peel and raisin-pineapple mixture.

➤ Pour puréed ingredients into slow cooker. Cover and cook on LOW 6 hours. Spoon pudding into 8 or 10 dessert dishes and serve hot. Garnish with mint.

Each serving contains:

Cal	Prot	Carb	Fat	Chol	Sodium
362	10g	60g	8g	65mg	345mg

Pork Roast with Fennel & Sage

Makes 5 or 6 servings

Be sure to buy a roast that will fit inside your slow cooker. Have the butcher cut roast through most of bone to form individual chops.

1 (3-lb.) pork loin roast	2 fennel bulbs, sliced crosswise
1/4 teaspoon salt	2 tablespoons cornstarch
1/8 teaspoon pepper	1/2 cup dry white wine
4 tablespoons chopped fresh sage	

➤ Trim off most of the fat on the roast. If necessary, tie roast to hold it together. Sprinkle top and sides with salt, pepper and fresh sage. Place on rack in slow cooker; top with fennel. Cover and cook on LOW 7 to 8 hours.

➤ Remove roast and most of fennel; keep warm.

➤ Turn slow cooker on HIGH. Dissolve cornstarch in wine. Stir into drippings. Cover and cook on HIGH 25 to 30 minutes or until thickened; stir once or twice.

➤ To serve, cut roast into chops. Spoon fennel over pork; then sauce over all.

 Also known as sweet anise, *fennel has a very mild licorice flavor.*

Each serving contains:

Cal	Prot	Carb	Fat	Chol	Sodium
444	50g	5g	22g	159mg	268mg

8 to 10 Hours

If you choose a recipe from this chapter, tantalizing aromas will permeate your home all day. These dishes require long slow-cooking to bring out the maximum flavor. Several soups and stews present a potpourri of flavors. Also included are hearty dishes, usually under the label of chili or stew, that are too thick to be called soups.

Savory Turkey Chowder

Makes 6 to 8 servings

This "comfort chowder" will soothe you on even the most hectic days.

I lb. lean ground turkey

2 sweet potatoes, peeled, diced

I parsnip, peeled, sliced

I large onion, peeled, thinly sliced

3 medium zucchini, sliced

I (46-oz.) can V-8® vegetable juice

I teaspoon ground savory

I teaspoon grated fresh ginger

Yogurt or sour cream, for garnish

➤ Turn slow cooker on HIGH. Add turkey; cook and stir until crumbly. (Or sauté turkey in a skillet and then place in slow cooker.)

➤ Add remaining ingredients. Turn slow cooker to LOW. Cover and cook on LOW for 8 to 9 hours. Garnish with a dollop of yogurt or sour cream.

Each serving contains:

Cal	Prot	Carb	Fat	Chol	Sodium
218	13g	23g	9g	53mg	680mg

Mahogany Leg of Lamb

Makes 6 to 8 servings

Here is a very different lamb dish that will win converts. Serve with broiled cherry tomatoes and cheesy mashed potatoes.

1 (3-1/3 to 4 lb.) boneless, rolled
   leg of lamb

1/2 cup strong coffee

1/4 cup curaçao

2 tablespoons dark brown sugar

2 tablespoons molasses

1/2 teaspoon ground cinnamon

1/2 teaspoon garlic powder

1/4 teaspoon ground mace

1/4 teaspoon black pepper

1 cup pitted prunes, cut in halves

2 tablespoons cornstarch

1/4 cup water

➤ Place lamb in slow cooker. In a bowl, combine remaining ingredients, except cornstarch and water, and pour over lamb. Cover and cook on LOW 8 to 9 hours or until meat is tender.

➤ Remove meat to serving platter. Turn slow cooker up to HIGH. For gravy, dissolve cornstarch in water and stir into pot juices and cook until slightly thickened. Serve with mashed potatoes.

Each serving contains:

Cal	Prot	Carb	Fat	Chol	Sodium
629	63g	51g	17g	194mg	156mg

Angel Hair Pasta Soup

Makes 8 to 10 servings

Other pastas may be substituted for the angel hair. Try cheese-filled ravioli or other fresh refrigerated pastas found in the deli or dairy section of your market.

1 onion, quartered	1 (28-oz.) can Italian-style tomatoes
1 medium celery root, peeled, cubed	2 oz. prosciutto ham, coarsely chopped
1 garlic clove	5 cups chicken broth or bouillon
1 teaspoon chopped fresh thyme	4 oz. angel hair (capellini) pasta, broken into 3- or 4-inch lengths
1 carrot, peeled, quartered	Grated Parmesan cheese
1 tablespoon coarsely chopped fresh parsley	

➤ In food processor fitted with metal blade, combine onion, celery root, garlic, thyme, carrot and parsley. Process until finely chopped but not puréed; remove. Repeat process with tomatoes and prosciutto.

➤ Combine chopped ingredients and broth or bouillon in slow cooker. Cover; cook on LOW 8 to 9 hours.

➤ Turn on HIGH. Add pasta; cover and cook on HIGH 20 to 25 minutes or until pasta is tender.

➤ Ladle into individual bowls; sprinkle with Parmesan cheese.

 Capellini (capelli d'angelo), which means angel hair, is the thinnest variety of pasta.

Each serving contains:

Cal	Prot	Carb	Fat	Chol	Sodium
98	7g	15g	2g	4mg	247mg

Vegetarian Lentil Chili

Makes 5 to 6 servings

For an interesting change, serve over baked potatoes.

2 carrots, shredded

1 small zucchini, chopped

1/2 cup pitted green olives

1 (14-1/2-oz.) can chopped, peeled tomatoes

1 (8-oz.) can tomato sauce

1 onion, chopped

1 garlic clove, crushed

1/2 teaspoon ground cumin

2 teaspoons chili powder

2 tablespoons chopped fresh cilantro leaves

2 tablespoons balsamic vinegar

1 cup dried lentils, rinsed

1/2 teaspoon salt

1/3 cup plain lowfat yogurt, stirred

Cilantro sprigs

➤ In slow cooker, combine all ingredients except yogurt and cilantro sprigs. Cover and cook on LOW 8 to 9 hours.

➤ Garnish with yogurt and cilantro sprigs.

 Lentils are available in colors varying from green to yellow, orange or brown. Presoaking is not necessary before cooking.

Each serving contains:

Cal	Prot	Carb	Fat	Chol	Sodium
274	29g	26g	6g	55mg	568mg

Potato Shitake Soup

Makes 9 cups

If you prefer, serve this soup without puréeing. It's equally delicious when it has lots of texture.

1 oz. dried shitake mushrooms, chopped

4 medium potatoes, peeled and cubed

1 small onion, diced

1 cup chopped uncooked chicken or turkey

6 cups chicken broth or bouillon

2 tablespoons chopped fresh celery leaves

1 teaspoon Worcestershire sauce

1/2 teaspoon salt

1/8 teaspoon pepper

Dairy sour cream

Fresh celery leaves for garnish

➤ In slow cooker, combine chopped mushrooms, potatoes, onions, chicken or turkey, broth or bouillon, 2 tablespoons celery leaves, Worcestershire sauce, salt and pepper. Cover and cook on LOW 8 to 9 hours or until potatoes are soft.

➤ Process, half at a time, in blender or food processor fitted with metal blade until finely chopped but not smooth.

➤ Garnish each serving with a dab of sour cream and celery leaves.

1 cup contains:

Cal	Prot	Carb	Fat	Chol	Sodium
118	9g	16g	2g	14mg	160mg

Gingered Carrot-Leek Vichyssoise

Makes about 6 servings

Instead of sour cream, add half-and-half or whipping cream to cooked mixture.

3 medium carrots, peeled, shredded

2 leeks, washed, sliced crosswise

3 potatoes, peeled, cubed

2 teaspoons grated fresh ginger root

1/4 teaspoon salt

1/8 teaspoon pepper

4 cups chicken broth or bouillon

1/2 cup dairy sour cream

Shredded carrot for garnish, optional

➤ In slow cooker, layer carrots, leeks and potatoes. Sprinkle with fresh ginger root, salt and pepper. Pour chicken broth or bouillon over all. Cover and cook on LOW 9 to 10 hours.

➤ Purée, half at a time, in blender or food processor fitted with metal blade. Gradually stir puréed mixture into sour cream.

➤ Reheat in microwave or on stovetop, if desired.

➤ Sprinkle shredded carrot on top, if desired.

Each serving contains:

Cal	Prot	Carb	Fat	Chol	Sodium
166	6g	25g	5g	9mg	122mg

Traditional Bolognese Sauce

Makes about 8 cups

Spoon this tasty sauce over any cooked pasta, including interesting shapes such as bow ties or spirals. Label and freeze excess sauce for another time.

I lb. lean ground beef

1/2 lb. Italian sausage, casing removed

I onion, chopped

I glove garlic, crushed

I small carrot, grated

2 stalks celery, chopped

I small green or red bell pepper, seeded, chopped

I (28-oz.) can diced, peeled tomatoes

2 (6-oz.) cans tomato paste

I teaspoon sugar

I tablespoon chopped fresh oregano

I tablespoon chopped fresh basil

I teaspoon salt

1/4 teaspoon pepper

1/2 cup dry red wine

Cooked pasta

Parmesan cheese, optional

➤ Turn slow cooker on HIGH. Add ground beef and sausage. Cook and stir until meat is broken up into small pieces.

➤ Turn pot on LOW. Add remaining ingredients, except pasta and cheese. Cover and cook on LOW 8 to 9 hours.

➤ Spoon over your favorite pasta. Sprinkle with grated Parmesan cheese, if desired.

 Bologna, Italy, is thought to be the birthplace of this versatile sauce.

I cup contains:

Cal	Prot	Carb	Fat	Chol	Sodium
253	17g	16g	14g	52mg	746mg

Mahogany Leg of Lamb, page 49

Traditional Bolognese Sauce, page 54

Creamy Greek Onion Soup

Makes about 8 cups

For more texture in your soup, process cooked vegetables until they're finely chopped but not smooth.

4 large onions, cut into 8ths

2 medium potatoes, peeled, cubed

1/4 cup margarine or butter

3 cups water

2 chicken bouillon cubes or
  2 teaspoons instant chicken
  granules

1/4 teaspoon pepper

2 cups milk or light cream

1/2 cup (2 oz.) herbed feta cheese,
  crumbled

➤ In slow cooker, combine onions, potatoes, margarine or butter, water, bouillon and pepper. Cover and cook on LOW 8 to 9 hours or until vegetables are tender.

➤ Purée, half at a time, in blender or food processor fitted with metal blade. Add milk or cream.

➤ Reheat to desired temperature in microwave or in saucepan on stove.

➤ Spoon into individual bowls. Top with feta cheese.

1 cup contains:

Cal	Prot	Carb	Fat	Chol	Sodium
136	5g	12g	8g	12mg	510mg

Lamb Ragout

Makes 6 to 7 servings

If cooked vegetables cool while you're thickening the sauce, reheat them in the microwave before returning to the slow cooker.

4 medium carrots, peeled, cut into crosswise slices

3 medium turnips, peeled, cut into 8ths

1-1/2 lb. lamb stew meat in 1-inch cubes

8 small new red potatoes, halved, not peeled

1 tablespoon chopped fresh parsley

1 garlic clove, crushed

1/2 teaspoon salt

1/8 teaspoon pepper

1 teaspoon chopped fresh marjoram

1 cup beef broth or bouillon

1/2 cup dry white wine

2 tablespoons cornstarch

3 tablespoons cold water

➤ Place carrots and turnips on bottom of slow cooker. Top with lamb and potatoes.

➤ In small bowl, combine parsley, garlic, salt, pepper, marjoram, broth or bouillon and wine. Pour over ingredients in pot. Cover and cook on LOW 8 to 9 hours.

➤ Turn pot on HIGH. Remove vegetables and meat with slotted spoon; keep warm.

➤ In small bowl, dissolve cornstarch in water. Stir into liquid in pot. Cover and cook on HIGH 15 to 20 minutes, stirring occasionally.

➤ Return vegetables and meat to pot; serve.

 Ragout *is the French term for a stew.*

Each serving contains:

Cal	Prot	Carb	Fat	Chol	Sodium
248	23g	22g	6g	65mg	253mg

Fresh Vegetable Soup with Pasta

Makes 6 or 7 servings

In this nutritious, good-tasting soup, beef broth enhances the flavor of fresh vegetables.

1 medium onion, chopped sliced	2 cups water
2 carrots, peeled, thinly sliced	2 tablespoons chopped fresh parsley
2 zucchini, sliced peeled	1 tablespoon chopped fresh oregano
2 medium tomatoes, peeled, seeded, chopped	1/2 cup small shell-shaped pasta
2 (10-1/2-oz.) cans condensed beef broth	Grated Parmesan cheese

➤ In slow cooker, combine onion, carrots, zucchini, tomatoes, condensed beef broth, water, parsley and oregano. Cover and cook on LOW 8 to 9 hours or until vegetables are tender.

➤ Turn on HIGH. Add pasta; cover and cook on HIGH 20 minutes or until pasta is tender.

➤ Ladle into serving bowls; sprinkle with cheese.

Each serving contains:

Cal	Prot	Carb	Fat	Chol	Sodium
61	3g	12g	1g	0mg	275mg

Southwestern Black Bean Soup

Makes 6 to 8 servings

A hearty bean soup paired with ham and herbs.

1 lb. dried black beans, rinsed	1 teaspoon ground oregano
6 cups beef broth or bouillon	1 teaspoon ground thyme
1 large onion, chopped	1/8 teaspoon ground cloves
2 jalapeño peppers, seeded, chopped	2 (about 1-lb. each) ham hocks
1 garlic clove, crushed	1/3 cup dairy sour cream or plain yogurt, optional
1 teaspoon ground cumin	Cilantro, garnish

➤ In slow cooker, combine dried beans, broth or bouillon, onions, jalapeño peppers, garlic, cumin, oregano, thyme, cloves and ham hocks. Cover and cook on LOW 9 to 10 hours or until beans are tender.

➤ Remove ham hocks; cool. Shred lean meat; discard skin, bones and fat.

➤ Return shredded lean ham to pot and reheat on HIGH, if necessary.

➤ Spoon mixture into individual soup bowls. Top each with sour cream, if using cilantro.

 In Puerto Rico, black bean soup is traditionally served with a dash of vinegar and a garnish of white rice and chopped egg.

Each serving contains:

Cal	Prot	Carb	Fat	Chol	Sodium
233	17g	29g	6g	15mg	247mg

Adriatic Cabbage Soup

Makes about 6 servings

A sprinkle of grated Romano cheese gives just the right finishing touch.

1/4 lb. salami, diced

1 carrot, peeled, finely chopped

1 garlic clove, crushed

3/4 cup diced ham

1 tablespoon white wine vinegar

1 cup thinly sliced fennel with some tops

4 cups water

1 small head (about 6 cups) savoy cabbage, thinly sliced

➤ In slow cooker, combine salami, carrot, garlic, ham, vinegar, fennel and water. Cover and cook on LOW 8 to 10 hours.

➤ Turn pot on HIGH; add cabbage. Cover and cook on HIGH 30 minutes or until cabbage is tender.

Each serving contains:

Cal	Prot	Carb	Fat	Chol	Sodium
104	9g	7g	5g	21mg	492mg

Today's Beef Stew

Makes 6 or 7 servings

This is a chance to use tender baby carrots, tiny white onions and unpeeled new potatoes.

10 (about 1/2 lb.) small new
potatoes, halved but not peeled

12 small white onions, peeled

30 (about 1/2 lb.) baby carrots

1 red or green bell pepper, cut into
1-inch pieces

1-1/2 lb. beef stew meat, cut into
1- to 1-1/2-inch cubes

2 cups beef broth or bouillon

2 teaspoons chopped fresh
oregano leaves

1/4 teaspoon paprika

1 tablespoon chopped fresh parsley

1 tablespoon Worcestershire sauce

1/2 teaspoon salt

1/8 teaspoon pepper

3 tablespoons cornstarch

3 tablespoons cold water

➤ Place potatoes, onions and baby carrots in slow cooker. Add bell pepper and beef.

➤ In small bowl, combine broth or bouillon, oregano, paprika, parsley, Worcestershire sauce, salt and pepper. Pour over meat and vegetables. Cover and cook on LOW 9 to 10 hours.

➤ Turn pot on HIGH. In small bowl, dissolve cornstarch in water; stir into cooked stew mixture. Cover and cook on HIGH 15 to 20 minutes or until thickened, stirring occasionally.

Each serving contains:

Cal	Prot	Carb	Fat	Chol	Sodium
229	25g	15g	7g	70mg	303mg

Lentil 'n' Ham Pot

Makes about 8 servings

Orange lentils and carrots produce a pretty as well as wholesome dish.

2 (about 8 to 10 oz. each)
  ham hocks

3 cups chicken broth or bouillon

2 cups water

1 small celery root, cut into
  2 by 1/2 by 1/4-inch slices

2 medium carrots, peeled,
  thinly sliced

1 leek, washed, sliced crosswise

1/2 small head cabbage, sliced

1 (8-oz.) can tomato sauce

1 garlic clove, crushed

1 teaspoon paprika

1 teaspoon chopped fresh marjoram

1/8 teaspoon pepper

1 cup dried lentils, rinsed

1/2 cup plain yogurt

➤ In slow cooker, combine all ingredients except yogurt. Cover and cook on LOW 9 to 10 hours or until vegetables and lentils are tender.

➤ Remove ham hocks; cool. Discard skin, bones and fat; cut lean meat into small pieces. Return lean meat to pot and reheat on HIGH, if necessary.

➤ Spoon into individual bowls; top with yogurt.

Each serving contains:

Cal	Prot	Carb	Fat	Chol	Sodium
186	15g	24g	4g	12mg	444mg

Spicy Kumquat Relish

Makes about 2 cups

This special recipe is designed for a 1-quart Crock-Ette®. If you double or triple the recipe and cook in a larger cooker, make sure the pot is half full.

2 cups (about 10 oz.) kumquats, sliced crosswise

1/2 cup dried-apple chips

2 tablespoons thinly sliced crystallized ginger

3/4 cup brown sugar

2 tablespoons honey

1/4 teaspoon ground allspice

2 tablespoons cider vinegar

1/4 cup golden raisins

1/4 teaspoon dried red-pepper flakes

1/2 cup coarsely chopped dried apricots

➤ In 1-quart slow cooker, combine all ingredients. Cover and cook on LOW 8 to 9 hours.

➤ Cool; serve as an accompaniment to pork or chicken.

 Wrapped in plastic, fresh kumquats will keep in the refrigerator for weeks.

1 tablespoon contains:

Cal	Prot	Carb	Fat	Chol	Sodium
44	0g	12g	0g	0mg	5mg

More Than 10 Hours

Beans are a nutritious, low-cost staple that can be used in numerous ways, such as in soups, stews, side dishes or main dishes. Traditionally, dried beans are associated with long cooking. Larger, denser varieties, like garbanzo or kidney beans, take the maximum time to cook, while lentils and black-eye peas cook in about half the time.

Preparation has been made easier by omitting overnight soaking. This works well, with the exception of recipes having a high sugar content. Note that *Sweet-Hot Bean Casserole* requires overnight soaking before slow cooking. Presoaking may reduce cooking time in high altitudes.

Slow cookers are ideal for making stock, so recipes are included for *Beef Stock* and *Chicken Stock* (with a vegetarian variation).

Tamale Soup

Makes 10 to 12 servings

Flavors of Mexico abound in this soup.

1 tablespoon olive oil

1 large onion, finely chopped

2 garlic cloves, minced

1-1/2 lb. chuck roast, chopped

1 (15-oz.) can tomato purée

2-1/2 cups tomato juice

1 (14-oz.) can beef broth

1/2 cup sliced black olives

1/2 cup canned chopped
   green chiles

1 (11-oz.) can kernel corn, drained

1 (10-oz.) pkg. frozen spinach,
   thawed, drained

1 jalapeño pepper, chopped

1 tablespoon chili powder

1 teaspoon cayenne pepper

1 large tomato, chopped

Salt and pepper, to taste

2 cups shredded cheddar cheese

2 cups corn chips

➤ Heat oil in a skillet and sauté onion, garlic and meat. Stir until meat is no longer pink.

➤ Place meat mixture and all remaining ingredients, except cheese and corn chips, in a 5-quart slow cooker. Cover and cook on LOW 10 to 12 hours. Serve topped with cheese and corn chips.

Each serving contains:

Cal	Prot	Carb	Fat	Chol	Sodium
311	25g	20g	16g	70mg	911mg

Traditional Baked Beans

Makes 6 to 8 servings

Good old-fashioned baked beans without soaking ahead of time. I like to start these the night before I plan to serve them.

1 lb. dried small white beans, rinsed	1 onion, chopped
4-1/2 cups water	1/4 lb. salt pork, cut into 1-inch cubes
1/3 cup molasses	1 tablespoon Dijon-style mustard
1/4 cup brown sugar	1/2 teaspoon salt

In slow cooker, combine all ingredients. Cover and cook on LOW 13 to 14 hours, stirring occasionally, if possible.

 For added nutrition, serve protein-rich beans with a grain such as rice or a multigrain or corn bread.

Each serving contains:

Cal	Prot	Carb	Fat	Chol	Sodium
299	15g	44g	8g	12mg	391mg

Amalfi Garbanzo Stew

Makes 6 to 8 servings

Use fresh basil and thyme to enhance the flavor of this delicious Italian stew.

1 lb. dried Garbanzo beans, rinsed

5 cups water

1 (6-oz.) can tomato paste

1/2 cup dry white wine

1 tablespoon chopped fresh basil
  or 1 teaspoon dried

1 garlic clove, crushed

2 carrots, peeled, sliced crosswise

1 teaspoon fresh thyme or
  1/4 teaspoon dried

1 green or yellow bell pepper,
  seeded, sliced

1/2 teaspoon salt

1/8 teaspoon pepper

3 chicken breast halves, boned,
  skinned, cut into 1/2 by 1-inch pieces

1 cup (4 oz.) shredded mozzarella
  cheese

4 thin slices pepperoni, chopped

➤ In slow cooker, combine dried beans, water, tomato paste, wine, basil, garlic, carrots, thyme, bell peppers, salt, pepper, pepperoni and chicken. Cover and cook on LOW 10 to 12 hours or until beans are tender.

➤ Spoon into individual bowls. Sprinkle with cheese and serve with a crusty bread.

Each serving contains:

Cal	Prot	Carb	Fat	Chol	Sodium
301	20g	38g	7g	23mg	296mg

Country Lima Bean & Cabbage Soup

Makes 8 to 9 servings

A robust dish high in fiber and low in fat. Red-pepper flakes provide extra flavor.

1 lb. dried baby lima beans, rinsed	1/2 teaspoon dried red-pepper flakes, crushed
8 cups chicken broth or bouillon	1/2 teaspoon salt
1 onion, chopped	1/8 teaspoon pepper
1 teaspoon chopped fresh marjoram	3 cups shredded cabbage
1 garlic clove, crushed	

➤ In slow cooker, combine all ingredients. Cover and cook on LOW 10 to 11 hours or until beans are tender.

➤ Ladle into individual bowls.

Each serving contains:

Cal	Prot	Carb	Fat	Chol	Sodium
144	12g	21g	2g	1mg	125mg

Sweet-Hot Bean Casserole

Makes 6 to 7 servings

Sweet-hot mustard and crushed gingersnaps create a wonderful sauce.

1 lb. dried great Northern beans, rinsed	1 tablespoon Worcestershire sauce
6 cups water	1/2 cup molasses
1 cup crushed gingersnaps (about 16)	3 green onions, chopped
2 tablespoons sweet-hot mustard	1/2 teaspoon salt
	1/8 teaspoon pepper

➤ In slow cooker, combine dried beans and water; let stand overnight or at least 8 hours. Drain; reserve 2-1/2 cups liquid from beans.

➤ In slow cooker, combine drained beans, reserved liquid, crushed gingersnaps, mustard, Worcestershire sauce, molasses, green onions, salt and pepper. Cover and cook on LOW about 10 hours.

 If possible, stir the beans once while they are cooking.

Each serving contains:

Cal	Prot	Carb	Fat	Chol	Sodium
339	12g	58g	7g	8mg	345mg

Irish Corned Beef Dinner

Makes 6 servings

Serve this traditional corned-beef dinner in the pot along with your favorite horseradish and mustard.

6 medium carrots, peeled,
cut into 1-inch lengths

6 medium potatoes, peeled,
quartered

2 turnips or parsnips, peeled,
cut into 8ths

2 large onions, peeled, quartered

1 bay leaf

1 tablespoon chopped chives

1/4 teaspoon ground allspice

1/4 teaspoon dry mustard

1 (2- to 3-lb.) corned-beef brisket

5 cups water

1 small head cabbage, cut into
6 wedges

➤ In slow cooker, combine carrots, potatoes, turnips or parsnips, onions, bay leaf, chives, allspice and mustard. Top with corned beef, fat-side up. Pour water over all. Cover and cook on LOW 10 to 11 hours or until meat is tender.

➤ Remove cooked meat and vegetables; keep warm. Turn pot on HIGH; add cabbage. Cover and cook on HIGH 20 to 30 minutes or until cabbage is done. Remove bay leaf.

➤ Lift cabbage with slotted spoon. Arrange on large platter with corned beef and other vegetables.

 You'll need a 4-quart or larger pot for this recipe, or use fewer vegetables in a smaller pot.

Each serving contains:

Cal	Prot	Carb	Fat	Chol	Sodium
406	43g	39g	9g	92mg	140mg

Garbanzo Meal-in-a-Pot

Makes about 8 servings

Put everything in the pot and forget about it until dinner time. These ingredients almost reach the top of a 3-1/2-quart slow cooker, but will cook perfectly.

1 lb. dried Garbanzo beans, rinsed

3 cups chicken broth or bouillon

3 cups water

4 large tomatoes, peeled, seeded, chopped

3/4 lb. lean pork, cut into 1/2-inch cubes

3 oz. prosciutto, chopped

1 onion, chopped

1 garlic clove, crushed

1 yellow or green bell pepper, seeded, chopped

2 teaspoons chopped fresh basil

1/2 teaspoon salt

1/8 teaspoon pepper

1 cup torn fresh spinach

In slow cooker, combine all ingredients. Cover and cook on LOW 10 to 11 hours or until beans are tender.

 Garbanzo beans are also known as chick peas, cei *or* chana dol. *They're a staple in Middle Eastern, European and Asian diets.*

Each serving contains:

Cal	Prot	Carb	Fat	Chol	Sodium
307	25g	36g	8g	38mg	322mg

Chicken Stock*

Makes about 7 cups

This flavorful stock can be frozen in 1- or 2-cup containers for later use in casseroles or soup.

3 lb. chicken necks, backs
  or wings

2 carrots, peeled, finely chopped

2 leeks, finely chopped

2 stalks celery with leaves,
  finely chopped

5 or 6 whole black peppercorns

1/4 cup loosely packed watercress

1 teaspoon fresh tarragon leaves

1 teaspoon salt

2 quarts water

➤ Arrange chicken in single layer in shallow roasting pan. Bake in 325F (165C) oven about 1 hour or until brown, turning pieces as they brown.

➤ Transfer browned chicken to slow cooker. Add remaining ingredients. Cover and cook on LOW 10 to 12 hours or until vegetables are very tender.

➤ Strain broth through fine sieve; discard vegetables and chicken. Refrigerate stock until cold; remove fat, if desired.

Vegetarian Stock: Omit chicken; add 6 mushrooms, chopped, and 1 bay leaf.

 To prevent bubbling over, do not fill slow cooker to the brim. If watercress is not available, use fresh parsley.

1 cup chicken stock contains:

Cal	Prot	Carb	Fat	Chol	Sodium
39	5g	1g	1g	1mg	305mg

1 cup vegetarian stock contains:

Cal	Prot	Carb	Fat	Chol	Sodium
34	1g	7g	0g	0mg	72mg

Beef Stock

Makes about 7 cups

Use bones with a small amount of meat on them to ensure a better beef flavor.

3 lb. beef bones	I teaspoon fresh thyme leave
2 carrots, peeled, finely chopped	5 or 6 black peppercorns
I medium onion, chopped	1/2 teaspoon salt
2 stalks celery with leaves, finely chopped	2 quarts water
2 bay leaves	

➤ Arrange single layer of bones in shallow roasting pan. Bake in 325F (165C) oven about 1 hour or until brown, turning bones as they brown.

➤ Transfer browned bones to slow cooker. Add remaining ingredients. Cover and cook on LOW 10 to 12 hours or until vegetables are very tender.

➤ Strain broth through fine strainer; discard herbs, vegetables, bones and meat. Refrigerate stock until cold; remove fat, if desired.

 Roasting the bones beforehand gives the stock a rich, deep color and better flavor.

I cup contains:

Cal	Prot	Carb	Fat	Chol	Sodium
16	3g	0g	Ig	Img	152mg

Slow Cooker Entertaining

The slow cooker makes an excellent serving container for hot punch or cider to welcome your guests. While you're busy with last-minute chores before entertaining, your slow cooker continues cooking unattended. It could be cooking a new hot appetizer, an exciting main dish or keeping foods warm that you've cooked in the microwave or on the stovetop.

It's possible to prepare festive, long-cooking fare the day before a party. Refrigerate the food overnight; then reheat it and keep it in a warm (on LOW) slow cooker throughout a buffet or cocktail party. You can rely on the food being just as warm for the last guest as it was for the first.

Banana-Blueberry Bread Pudding

Makes 6 servings

A wonderful way to turn leftover bread into a warm dessert.

5-1/2 cups cinnamon bread, cubed

1/2 cup light brown sugar

1/4 teaspoon salt

1/4 teaspoon ground cinnamon

2 eggs, beaten

2 cups milk or half-and-half, warmed

1/2 teaspoon vanilla, extract

1 large banana, chopped

1 cup fresh, canned or frozen blueberries, drained

1/2 cup chopped pecans or walnuts

Vanilla Sauce

1 (3-oz.) pkg. vanilla pudding and pie mix

3 cups milk

Whipped cream, for garnish

➤ Butter a 2-quart bowl or mold, set aside.

➤ In a large bowl, thoroughly combine ingredients. Spoon mixture into prepared bowl or mold; cover with foil.

➤ Place a trivet or metal rack in the bottom of a 4-quart or larger slow cooker. Pour in 2 cups hot water. Place bowl or mold in slow cooker. Cover and cook on HIGH 2 to 3 hours.

➤ Remove and serve warm or cold, topped with Vanilla Sauce and whipped cream.

Vanilla Sauce: Cook pudding according to package directions, using 3 cups milk. The sauce will be thin.

Each serving contains:

Cal	Prot	Carb	Fat	Chol	Sodium
509	12g	58g	28g	127mg	517mg

Turkey Marsala with Vegetables

Makes 5 or 6 servings

If your slow cooker is large enough to accommodate a whole turkey breast, consider this dish.

3 large carrots, peeled, julienned

2 leeks, washed, julienned

1/2 (about 3 lb.) turkey breast, skinned

2 tablespoons melted margarine or butter

12 mushrooms, sliced

1/2 teaspoon salt

1/8 teaspoon pepper

2 tablespoons chopped fresh parsley

3/4 cup chicken broth or bouillon

1/2 cup Marsala or dry sherry

2 tablespoons cornstarch

2 tablespoons cold water

➤ Place carrots and leeks in slow cooker. Brush turkey breast with melted margarine or butter. Arrange turkey, then mushrooms over vegetables. Sprinkle with salt, pepper and parsley. Pour broth or bouillon and wine over all. Cover and cook on LOW 6 to 7 hours.

➤ Remove turkey and vegetables with slotted spoon; cover and keep warm.

➤ Turn pot on HIGH. Dissolve cornstarch in water. Stir into juices in pot. Cover and cook on HIGH 15 to 20 minutes or until thickened, stirring occasionally.

➤ Slice turkey; arrange on center of platter with vegetables around edges. Serve with Marsala sauce.

Each serving contains:

Cal	Prot	Carb	Fat	Chol	Sodium
287	36g	13g	7g	79mg	321mg

Peppercorn Pork

Makes 6 to 8 servings

Buy a pork roast that will fit the size of your slow cooker. Some large roasts won't fit into a 3-1/2 quart pot.

2 tablespoons green peppercorns, drained

3 tablespoons sweet-hot mustard

1 teaspoon horseradish

1/2 teaspoon grated lemon peel

1/4 teaspoon salt

3-1/2 to 4 lb. boneless, lean pork roast

1 cup apple cider

1/4 cup cold water

3 tablespoons cornstarch

1 apple, cored, cut into thin wedges

➤ In small bowl, combine peppercorns, mustard, horseradish, lemon peel and salt. Spread on top and sides of pork roast.

➤ Place metal rack in bottom of slow cooker; pour in cider. Place coated pork roast on rack in slow cooker. Cover and cook on LOW 9 to 10 hours.

➤ Then turn slow cooker on HIGH. Remove pork and rack; cover and keep warm. In small bowl, combine water and cornstarch; stir until smooth. Add to drippings in pot. Cook on HIGH 20 to 30 minutes or until thickened, stirring occasionally.

➤ Slice roast; garnish with apple wedges. Serve pork with sauce.

Each serving contains:

Cal	Prot	Carb	Fat	Chol	Sodium
396	44g	8g	20g	139mg	240mg

Flank Steak Pinwheels

Makes 8 steak pinwheels

Smaller slow cookers (3-1/2- or 4-quart) are the ideal size for this recipe.

1 (about 1-1/2-lb.) beef flank steak	1 garlic clove, crushed
2 tablespoons chutney	1/4 teaspoon salt
1 tablespoon soy sauce	1/8 teaspoon pepper
1 tablespoon white wine vinegar	Cooked rice or noodles
1 tablespoon vegetable oil	

➤ Trim all fat off flank steak; cut into 8 crosswise strips. Roll up; secure with small wooden pick. Place in bottom of slow cooker.

➤ In small bowl, combine chutney, soy sauce, vinegar, oil, garlic, salt and pepper. Spoon over steak pinwheels. Cover and cook on LOW about 6 hours or until tender.

➤ Remove wooden picks. Serve pinwheels and the meat juices over cooked rice or noodles.

1 pinwheel contains:

Cal	Prot	Carb	Fat	Chol	Sodium
150	17g	1g	8g	43mg	281mg

Sicilian Hens on Fettuccine

Makes 4 servings

Tender Cornish hens flavored with capers give an Italian accent.

1/4 cup toasted sliced almonds	1/2 teaspoon salt
3 tablespoons drained capers	1/8 teaspoon pepper
3 tablespoons chopped fresh parsley	2 Cornish hens, thawed, halved
1 garlic clove, chopped	Cooked fettuccine
1/2 teaspoon paprika	Chopped ripe olives
2 teaspoons olive or vegetable oil	

➤ In food processor fitted with metal blade, combine almonds, capers, parsley, garlic, paprika, oil, salt and pepper. Process until finely chopped but not puréed. Pat mixture on all sides of Cornish hens.

➤ Place on rack in slow cooker. If hens do not fit on rack, place 2 halves on rack; lightly cover with heavy-duty foil. Arrange remaining halves on top of foil. Cover and cook on LOW 7 to 8 hours.

➤ Serve on fettuccine; sprinkle with chopped ripe olives.

 Capers, the pickled flower buds of Mediterranean shrubs, vary in size and color.

Each serving contains:

Cal	Prot	Carb	Fat	Chol	Sodium
234	32g	1g	11g	94mg	484mg

Herb-Stuffed Turkey Breast

Makes 6 to 8 servings

Fresh sage and parsley make attractive garnishes for cooked turkey slices.

1 (2-1/4- to 2-1/2-lb.) half turkey breast, boned, with skin

1 tablespoon Dijon-style mustard

6 thin slices (about 1/2 lb.) Canadian bacon

4 to 5 fresh sage leaves

1 tablespoon chopped fresh parsley

1/4 teaspoon salt

1/8 teaspoon pepper

1 tablespoon cornstarch

1/4 cup dry white wine

➤ Place turkey breast skin-side down. Spread cut surfaces with mustard; top with Canadian bacon, sage and parsley.

➤ Fold long sides of breast over stuffing so they overlap slightly. Skewer or tie to hold sides together. Sprinkle with salt and pepper. Place skin-side up on rack in slow cooker. Cover and cook on LOW about 6 hours.

➤ Remove turkey and rack from pot; let juices remain. Keep covered and warm. Turn pot on HIGH. Dissolve cornstarch in wine. Stir into drippings in pot. Cover and cook on HIGH 20 to 30 minutes or until thickened, stirring occasionally.

➤ Remove skewer or tie from turkey. Slice turkey crosswise into 3/8- or 1/2-inch slices. Spoon wine sauce over slices.

 If fresh herbs are not available, substitute 1 teaspoon dried for each tablespoon fresh.

Each serving contains:

Cal	Prot	Carb	Fat	Chol	Sodium
241	43g	1g	6g	99mg	443mg

Italian Roll-Ups

Makes 6 servings

If you want to make something impressive, these roll-ups are it.

1/4 cup pine nuts, coarsely chopped

1 garlic clove, minced

2 tablespoons chopped fresh parsley

2 tablespoons chopped fresh basil

1 tablespoon olive or vegetable oil

1/4 teaspoon salt

1/8 teaspoon pepper

1-1/2-lb. boneless round steak, about 1/2 inch thick

6 slices proscuitto, well trimmed

1 cup beef broth or bouillon

1 oz. dried porcini or shitake mushrooms

1/2 cup dry red wine

2 tablespoons cornstarch

1/4 cup cold water

Pine nuts

➤ In small bowl, combine 1/4 cup chopped pine nuts, garlic, parsley, basil, oil, salt and pepper.

➤ Remove most of fat from steak. Cut into 6 pieces about 3 inches by 4 inches. Pound to about 1/4-inch thickness or 4 inches by 6 inches.

➤ Place a slice of proscuitto on each slice of pounded round steak. Spoon about 1 tablespoon herb mixture on each. Roll up like a jelly roll. Tie with string. Place on bottom of slow cooker.

➤ Heat broth or bouillon to boiling. Pour over dried mushrooms. Add to cooker. Pour in wine. Cover; cook on LOW 6 to 7 hours.

➤ Remove meat; cover and keep warm. Turn pot on HIGH. Dissolve cornstarch in water. Stir into liquid in pot. Cover; cook on HIGH 15 to 20 minutes. Spoon over roll-ups. Garnish with more pine nuts.

Each serving contains:

Cal	Prot	Carb	Fat	Chol	Sodium
326	36g	7g	15g	101mg	395mg

Sorrento Chicken

Makes 6 servings

For a smoother sauce, blend thickened broth in food processor before serving.

1 tablespoon Dijon-style mustard	1-1/2 oz. proscuitto, cut into 6 (1 by 9-inch) strips
1/2 teaspoon chopped fresh tarragon	1 cup fresh pearl onions, peeled
1 teaspoon minced fresh chives	1/2 cup dry white wine
1/4 teaspoon salt	1/2 cup chicken broth or bouillon
1/8 teaspoon pepper	1 cup seasoned croutons
6 chicken breast halves, boned, skinned	

➤ Combine mustard, tarragon, chives, salt and pepper. Spread on chicken breasts. Wrap strip of proscuitto around each.

➤ Place rack in bottom of slow cooker. Add onions; top with wrapped chicken. Combine wine and chicken broth or bouillon; pour over all. Cover and cook on LOW 5 to 6 hours or until chicken is tender.

➤ Remove chicken, onions and rack; cover and keep warm. Turn pot on HIGH. Pulverize croutons in food processor until they look like brown sugar. Stir into broth mixture. Cover and cook on HIGH 15 to 20 minutes or until thickened. Spoon over cooked chicken breasts.

1 cup contains:

Cal	Prot	Carb	Fat	Chol	Sodium
124	17g	5g	2g	41mg	315mg

Mediterranean Ratatouille

Makes 6 to 8 servings as a main dish;
20 to 25 as a dip

A versatile recipe that can serve as a hot main dish, side dish or cold appetizer.

1 large eggplant, peeled, cubed	1 garlic clove, crushed
2 tomatoes, peeled, seeded, cubed	1/4 cup chopped fresh cilantro leaves
3 zucchini, cubed	2 tablespoons chopped fresh basil
1 small onion, chopped	1/2 teaspoon salt
1 yellow bell pepper, cubed	1/4 teaspoon pepper
1/4 cup vegetable oil	Pita bread, cut into wedges

➤ Combine eggplant, tomatoes, zucchini, onion and bell pepper in slow cooker.

➤ In small bowl, combine oil, garlic, cilantro, basil, salt and pepper. Add to vegetables in pot. Cover and cook on LOW 7 to 8 hours or until vegetables are tender.

➤ Keep warm in the slow cooker and serve as a hearty vegetable dip or appetizer with pita bread.

1 cup contains:

Cal	Prot	Carb	Fat	Chol	Sodium
91	1g	7g	7g	0mg	140mg

Black Bean-Jalapeño Mousse

Makes 8 or 10 servings

If your digestive system is jalapeño-friendly, use two jalapeño peppers.

6 slices bacon, chopped
1 lb. dried black beans, rinsed
1 jalapeño pepper, seeded,
    chopped
1/2 teaspoon salt
1/4 teaspoon pepper
1 (10-1/2-oz.) can beef broth
1 teaspoon instant beef bouillon
1 cup red-wine vinegar
1 cup dry red wine
1 cup water
8 oz. smoked ham, diced

1 cup chopped fresh cilantro
1 large onion, chopped
2 envelopes unflavored gelatin
1/3 cup cold water

Goat Cheese Topping:
5 oz. goat cheese
1/4 cup dairy sour cream
1/3 cup nonfat milk
2 green onions, chopped
Stuffed green olives and fresh
    cilantro sprigs

➤ Sauté bacon until crisp, drain; set aside. Rinse beans; drain. Pour beans into slow cooker. Top with jalapeño pepper, salt and pepper.

➤ In 3- or 4-quart saucepan, combine beef broth, bouillon, vinegar, wine, 1 cup water, ham, chopped cilantro, onion and bacon. Cover and cook on medium-high until mixture boils. Pour into slow cooker; stir. Cover and cook on HIGH 6 hours.

➤ When beans are tender, sprinkle gelatin over 1/3 cup water. When softened, stir into hot beans. Spray 8-inch springform pan with cooking spray. Purée half of bean mixture at a time. Pour into springform pan; cover and refrigerate until firm. Prepare Goat Cheese Topping, recipe below.

Goat Cheese Topping: Thoroughly combine cheese, sour cream, milk and green onions. Cover and refrigerate.

➤ To serve, remove side of springform pan; cut into wedges. Top with Goat Cheese Topping; garnish with olives and cilantro.

Each serving contains:

Cal	Prot	Carb	Fat	Chol	Sodium
272	21g	25g	9g	35mg	833mg

Persimmon Pudding

Makes 6 to 8 servings

Bright orange, fig-shaped Hachiya persimmons should be very soft; the reddish-orange, tomato-shaped Fuyu can be slightly firm.

1-1/2 cups all-purpose flour	1/4 cup melted margarine or butter
1 cup sugar	1/2 cup chopped raisins
1 teaspoon baking powder	1/4 cup chopped pecans
1 teaspoon baking soda	***Hot Citrus Sauce:***
1 teaspoon cinnamon	2 tablespoons cornstarch
1/4 teaspoon nutmeg	1/2 cup sugar
2 persimmons	1/2 cup water
1 tablespoon lemon juice	1/2 cup orange juice
1/3 cup milk	2 tablespoons margarine
1 egg	1/4 teaspoon grated lemon peel
2 tablespoons honey	3 tablespoons lemon juice

➤ Grease 6- or 8-cup heat-proof mold. In large bowl, combine flour, sugar, baking powder, soda, cinnamon and nutmeg; set aside.

➤ Cut persimmons in half; scoop out pulp. Purée lemon juice and pulp in blender or food processor fitted with metal blade. Add milk, egg, honey and margarine; process until well blended. Stir liquid into flour mixture. Add raisins and nuts.

➤ Spoon into mold; cover. Place on rack in slow cooker. Pour in boiling water until it comes halfway up sides of mold. Cover and steam on HIGH 3 hours.

➤ Loosen sides by inserting a knife between pudding and sides of mold. Invert on a platter. Serve with Hot Citrus Sauce.

Hot Citrus Sauce: In small saucepan, combine cornstarch and sugar. Add water and orange juice; stir until smooth. Cook until thickened and translucent. Remove from heat. Add margarine, lemon peel and juice; stir. Makes about 1-1/2 cups.

Each serving with sauce contains:

Cal	Prot	Carb	Fat	Chol	Sodium
414	5g	80g	10g	28mg	266mg

Holiday Cran-Apple Sauce

Makes about 3-1/2 cups

This versatile dish works equally well as an accompaniment to poultry, dessert or breakfast fruit.

1 cup fresh cranberries	1 stick cinnamon, halved crosswise
8 apples, peeled, cored, chopped	6 whole cloves
1/2 cup sugar	Ground nutmeg

➤ Combine cranberries, apples and sugar in slow cooker.

➤ Place cinnamon and cloves in center of a 6-inch square of cheesecloth. Pull up around sides; tie to form pouch. Place in pot. Cover and cook on LOW 4 to 5 hours or until cranberries and apples are very soft.

➤ Remove spice bag. Purée hot fruit in blender or food processor fitted with metal blade. Sprinkle with nutmeg.

1 tablespoon contains:

Cal	Prot	Carb	Fat	Chol	Sodium
18	0g	5g	0g	0mg	0mg

Punch-of-Gold

Makes 15 to 18 servings

Ideal for buffet serving, here's the easiest punch you'll ever make.

2 (12-oz.) cans apricot nectar	3 pieces crystallized ginger, halved
1 quart orange juice	2 cinnamon sticks
1/4 cup orange liqueur	Fresh mint leaves
2 (12-oz.) cans mango nectar	

➤ In slow cooker, combine all ingredients except mint leaves. Cover; cook on LOW 4 or 5 hours.

➤ With slotted spoon, remove ginger and cinnamon sticks. Keep slow cooker on LOW. Serve warm in punch cups or coffee mugs; garnish with mint leaves.

Each serving contains:

Cal	Prot	Carb	Fat	Chol	Sodium
82	1g	18g	0g	0mg	3mg

Vegetarian Split-Pea Soup, page 25

Southwestern Black Bean Soup, page 58

Honey-Buttered Cranberry Cider

Makes 12 to 15 servings

Try this bright, vibrantly flavored beverage. The slow cooker keeps it hot until guests are ready for it.

1 (48-oz.) bottle cranberry juice cocktail

1 quart apple juice or cider

4 thin strips orange peel, about 2 inches long

1/3 cup margarine or butter

1/4 cup honey

1/2 teaspoon ground coriander

➤ In slow cooker, combine cranberry juice, apple juice or cider and orange peel. Cover and heat on LOW 5 to 7 hours.

➤ Just before serving, melt margarine or butter, honey and coriander in small saucepan or in microwave. Spoon slightly more than 1/2 tablespoon honey-margarine mixture in mug or heat-proof cup; add about 3/4 cup hot cranberry mixture. Serve immediately.

Each serving contains:

Cal	Prot	Carb	Fat	Chol	Sodium
127	0g	25g	3g	0mg	54mg

Fiesta Black-Bean Dip

Makes about 2-1/2 cups

For a spicy taste, guests can add a bit of fresh or bottled salsa on each chip.

1 cup dried black beans, rinsed

1 quart water

1 onion, chopped

1 garlic clove, crushed

1/4 cup chopped fresh cilantro

1/4 teaspoon salt

1 fresh jalapeño pepper, seeded, chopped

1/4 lb. salt pork, coarsely chopped

2 or 3 oz. goat cheese, crumbled

Fresh cilantro leaves for garnish

Taco or tortilla chips

Salsa, optional

➤ In slow cooker, combine dried beans, water, onion, garlic, 1/4 cup chopped cilantro, salt, jalapeño pepper and salt pork. Cover and cook on LOW 9 to 10 hours or until beans are soft. Drain; discard water.

➤ In blender or food processor fitted with metal blade, process drained bean mixture until almost smooth.

➤ Spoon into serving bowl. Sprinkle cheese and fresh cilantro leaves over top. Dip chips into bean mixture. Top with salsa, if desired.

1 tablespoon contains:

Cal	Prot	Carb	Fat	Chol	Sodium
24	1g	2g	1g	2mg	55mg

Round-the-World Flavors

For recipes in this chapter, I borrowed traditional flavors from other parts of the world. After all, good cooks in Europe have been slow cooking for centuries. Early versions of slow cookers were not electric, but heavy iron pots that simmered on the back of the stove or on the edge of a fireplace.

My round-the-world recipes are not authentic replicas of ethnic or regional dishes, but reflect favorite flavor combinations, traditional for generations, that have been adapted for use in slow cooking.

Thai Paradise Pork

Makes 6 servings

Tropical flavors of orange and coconut accent tender pork strips.

1 teaspoon ground cinnamon

1 teaspoon ground cloves

1 teaspoon ground nutmeg

4 boneless pork strips, about
    1 to 1-1/2 lb.

1/2 cup flaked coconut

1 cup unsweetened coconut milk

1/4 cup peanut butter

1 cup raisins or chopped dates

4 thin slices fresh orange

1/4 cup sliced almonds

➤ In a plastic bag, combine cinnamon, cloves, and nutmeg. Add pork and shake to coat. Place pork in one layer in slow cooker. Sprinkle coconut over all.

➤ In a bowl, combine coconut milk, peanut butter, raisins or dates and pour over meat. Place orange slices on top. Cover and cook on LOW 5 to 6 hours. To serve, spoon sauce over meat and top with almonds.

Each serving contains:

Cal	Prot	Carb	Fat	Chol	Sodium
460	16g	31g	32g	40mg	883mg

Spicy Indian Lamb Curry

Makes 6 servings

Create a party dish by accenting this delicious combination of fruits and lamb with chopped peanuts and chutney.

2 slices bacon, chopped

3 cloves garlic, minced

2 lb. lean boneless lamb, cubed

1 cup finely chopped onion

2 large Granny Smith apples, peeled, chopped

1/2 cup golden raisins

1/2 cup dried apricots, quartered

1 (15-oz.) can cannellini beans

1 teaspoon ground ginger

1 teaspoon dry mustard

1/2 teaspoon salt

1 tablespoon curry powder

2 tablespoons all-purpose flour

1/4 teaspoon black pepper

1/4 teaspoon red-pepper flakes

3/4 cup red wine

1 beef bouillon cube or 1 teaspoon beef granules

2 teaspoons lemon juice

➤ In a slow cooker, combine bacon, garlic, lamb, onion, raisins, apricots and beans. In a cup, blend together ginger, mustard, salt, curry powder, flour, black pepper and red pepper flakes.

➤ Sprinkle spice mixture over ingredients in slow cooker; stir to distribute evenly. Stir in remaining ingredients. Cover and cook over low heat 5 to 6 hours. If possible, stir occasionally.

Each serving contains:

Cal	Prot	Carb	Fat	Chol	Sodium
459	38g	45g	13g	102mg	677mg

Tamale Pie

Makes 6 or 7 servings

When serving, be sure to include part of the cornmeal lining in addition to the meat mixture in the center.

2 cups chicken broth or bouillon
1 cup yellow cornmeal
1 tablespoon chopped fresh cilantro
1/2 lb. pork sausage
1 lb. beef stew meat, cut into
   1/2-inch cubes
1 onion, chopped
1/2 cup finely chopped celery
1 mild green chile pepper, seeded,
   chopped

1/2 cup chopped sun-dried tomatoes
1 (8-oz.) can whole-kernel corn,
   drained
1 (2-1/2-oz.) can sliced ripe olives,
   drained
1/2 teaspoon salt
1/8 teaspoon pepper
Whole or halved pitted ripe olives,
   optional

➤ Bring broth or bouillon to boil in medium saucepan. Stirring constantly, slowly add cornmeal. Simmer mixture 5 minutes, stirring occasionally. Stir in cilantro.

➤ Using a greased spatula, spread cornmeal mixture on bottom and about 2 inches up sides of slow cooker.

➤ In large bowl, combine sausage, stew meat, onion, celery, chile pepper, sun-dried tomatoes, corn, sliced olives, salt and pepper. Carefully spoon into center of cornmeal-lined pot. Cover and cook on LOW 7 to 8 hours. Garnish with ripe olives, if desired.

 Do not remove cover during cooking because heat escapes quickly.

Each serving contains:

Cal	Prot	Carb	Fat	Chol	Sodium
372	24g	24g	20g	69mg	566mg

Aegean Lamb & Eggplant

Makes 4 to 5 servings

Lamb and eggplant, plus intriguing accents of sun-dried tomatoes and feta cheese, are combined in one great dish.

1 small eggplant, peeled, cut into 1-inch cubes

1 small onion, chopped

1/4 cup sun-dried tomatoes in oil, chopped

1/4 teaspoon dried red-pepper flakes

1 tablespoon balsamic vinegar

1/4 teaspoon salt

1 tablespoon chopped fresh basil

1 lb. lamb stew meat, cut into 2 by 1/2-inch strips

Cooked fettuccine

Feta cheese, crumbled

Fresh basil leaves

➤ In slow cooker, combine eggplant, onion, sun-dried tomatoes, red-pepper flakes, vinegar, salt, basil and lamb. Cover; cook on LOW 5 to 6 hours or until lamb is tender.

➤ Remove from cooker; spoon over cooked fettuccine. Top with crumbled feta cheese. Garnish with fresh basil leaves.

Each serving contains:

Cal	Prot	Carb	Fat	Chol	Sodium
195	19g	4g	11g	61mg	156mg

Thai Chicken Salad

Makes 5 or 6 servings

A colorful main-dish salad to enjoy any time of the year.

1 (2-1/2- to 3-lb.) chicken
1 cup chicken broth
1/2 teaspoon dry red-pepper flakes
1/2 teaspoon seasoned salt
1 tablespoon chopped fresh chives
1 cup snow peas
1 (8-oz.) can sliced water
    chestnuts, drained
1 red bell pepper, thinly sliced
1/4 cup vegetable oil

1 tablespoon sesame oil
1 tablespoon lime juice
2 tablespoons white-wine vinegar
1 tablespoon soy sauce
2 teaspoons finely chopped
    fresh ginger root
Tabasco® sauce
1 garlic clove, crushed
1 orange, peeled, sliced
1/4 cup salted peanuts

➤ Cut chicken in pieces; place in slow cooker. In small bowl, combine broth, red-pepper flakes, seasoned salt and chives. Pour over chicken. Cover and cook on LOW 4 to 5 hours or until chicken is done.

➤ Cool; remove meat from bones. Cut meat into bite-size pieces. Discard bones; use broth for soup or stew. Blanch snow peas; cool.

➤ In large bowl, combine chicken, snow peas, water chestnuts and bell pepper. In small bowl, combine oils, lime juice, vinegar, soy sauce, ginger root, 3 or 4 dashes of Tabasco® and garlic. Add to chicken mixture; toss. Top with orange slices and sprinkle with chopped peanuts just before serving.

 Thai foods are often fragrant with spicy surprises and are always beautifully presented.

Each serving contains:

Cal	Prot	Carb	Fat	Chol	Sodium
355	30g	12g	21g	79mg	446mg

Minestrone Napoli

Makes 10 cups

A satisfying and delicious soup hearty enough to be used as a main dish.

3 large tomatoes, peeled, seeded, chopped

1 bunch green onions, chopped

2 medium carrots, peeled, chopped

1/4 cup chopped fresh parsley

1 garlic clove, crushed

2 tablespoons chopped fresh basil leaves

1 (15-oz.) can red kidney beans, drained

2 zucchini, sliced

2 cups shredded cabbage

1/2 teaspoon chopped fresh oregano

1/2 teaspoon salt

1/8 teaspoon pepper

5 cups beef broth or bouillon

1/4 cup dry red wine

2 cups cooked small elbow pasta

1/4 cup grated Parmesan cheese, optional

➤ In slow cooker, combine tomatoes, green onions, carrots, parsley, garlic, basil, kidney beans, zucchini, cabbage, oregano, salt, pepper, broth and wine. Cover and cook on LOW 8 to 9 hours.

➤ Stir in cooked pasta. Sprinkle with cheese, if desired.

1 cup contains:

Cal	Prot	Carb	Fat	Chol	Sodium
113	6g	21g	1g	0mg	265mg

Greek Isles Pita Pockets

Makes 8 to 10 servings

Keep the cooked, shredded meat in your slow cooker so everyone can assemble his or her own pita pocket.

1-1/2 lb. lamb stew meat, cut into 1-inch cubes

3/4 lb. banana squash, peeled, cut into 1-inch cubes

1 medium red onion, diced

1/2 cup sliced celery

1/2 teaspoon salt

1 jalapeño pepper, seeded, minced

1 cube chicken bouillon, crushed or 1 teaspoon bouillon granules

1 garlic clove, crushed

1/8 teaspoon ground cumin

1/8 teaspoon ground coriander

8 to 10 pita bread rounds

8 to 10 lettuce leaves

1/4 cup plain yogurt

1/4 cup (1 oz.) feta cheese, crumbled

➤ In slow cooker, combine lamb, squash, onion, celery, salt, jalapeño pepper, bouillon, garlic, cumin and coriander. Cover and cook on LOW 8 to 9 hours or until meat is very tender.

➤ Strain mixture. Reserve about 1/4 cup broth; use remaining broth for soup or stew, if desired. Process drained cooked-meat mixture with reserved 1/4 cup broth in food processor until shredded.

➤ Cut about 1 inch off top of each pita round. Insert lettuce leaf into each. Spoon in meat mixture and yogurt. Top with cheese.

 Use caution when working with jalapeño or chile peppers. They can irritate your skin. Wear rubber gloves for protection, if you have sensitive skin.

Each serving contains:

Cal	Prot	Carb	Fat	Chol	Sodium
309	24g	38g	7g	54mg	654mg

Neopolitan Tostada

Makes 8 servings

Halve each pita round horizontally to form two rounds, then toast just before serving.

3/4 lb. ground turkey

1 eggplant, cubed (2-1/2 to 3 cups)

1 cup fresh or canned salsa

1 (6-oz.) can tomato paste

1/4 cup chopped fresh parsley

1 tablespoon chili powder

1 teaspoon ground cumin

1 teaspoon dried oregano

1 (10-oz.) pkg. frozen corn, thawed

4 pita rounds, halved, toasted

1/2 cup plain lowfat yogurt

2 cups shredded lettuce

1/2 cup sliced ripe olives

1/2 cup shredded cheese, optional

➤ Combine turkey, eggplant, salsa, tomato paste, parsley, chili powder, cumin, oregano and corn in slow cooker. Cover and cook on LOW 5 to 6 hours.

➤ Stir with a fork to break up large chunks of turkey. Spoon about 3/4 cup cooked turkey mixture on each pita half. Top with yogurt, lettuce, olives and cheese, if desired.

Each serving contains:

Cal	Prot	Carb	Fat	Chol	Sodium
256	16g	34g	8g	26mg	328mg

Old World Goulash

Makes 6 to 7 servings

Flavors borrowed from our European heritage create this hearty dish.

1-1/2 lb. boneless beef chuck,
   cut into 1-inch cubes

1 onion, sliced

2 teaspoons paprika

1/4 teaspoon salt

1/8 teaspoon pepper

1/2 cup beef broth or bouillon

2 medium potatoes, peeled, shredded

1 (14-oz.) can sauerkraut, drained

1 tablespoon brown sugar

1/4 teaspoon caraway seeds

1/2 cup plain lowfat yogurt or
   dairy sour cream

➤ In slow cooker, combine beef and onion. Sprinkle with paprika, salt and pepper. Pour broth or bouillon over all. Top with shredded potatoes, sauerkraut, brown sugar and caraway seeds. Cover and cook on LOW 8 to 9 hours.

➤ Turn off heat; stir in yogurt or sour cream.

Each serving contains:

Cal	Prot	Carb	Fat	Chol	Sodium
265	25g	14g	12g	78mg	517mg

Provençale Ratatouille

Makes 7 to 8 servings

A cross between a stew and a soup, this recipe contains some favorite flavors of southern France.

1 eggplant, peeled, cut into 1/2-inch cubes	1 jalapeño pepper
3 zucchini, cut into 1/2-inch slices	1 tablespoon chopped fresh basil
1 medium onion, sliced	1/4 teaspoon salt
2 medium tomatoes	1 tablespoon minced parsley
1 large green bell pepper	1/2 lb. smoked link sausage, thinly sliced
1 large yellow bell pepper	2 cups chicken broth or bouillon

➤ Combine eggplant, zucchini and onion in slow cooker.

➤ With sharp knife, make an X in skin at smooth end of tomatoes. Drop in boiling water for about 15 seconds; pull off skin. Halve and remove tomato and bell pepper seeds. Cut tomatoes and bell peppers in 1/2-inch pieces; seed and finely chop jalapeño pepper.

➤ Add tomatoes, peppers, basil, salt, parsley, smoked sausage and broth or bouillon to slow cooker. Stir; cover and cook on LOW 4 to 6 hours.

Each serving contains:

Cal	Prot	Carb	Fat	Chol	Sodium
138	6g	8g	9g	20mg	357mg

Brazilian Feijoada

Makes 10 to 12 servings

Not quite as elaborate as the traditional dish of Brazil, but with similar flavors.

1 lb. dried black beans, rinsed

1 medium onion, chopped

1 garlic clove, crushed

2 tomatoes, peeled, seeded, chopped

1 tablespoon chopped jalapeño pepper

1 tablespoon chopped fresh parsley

1/4 lb. Canadian bacon in one piece

3 or 4 oz. beef jerky, cut each into 12ths

1 lb. smoked sausage links, cut each into 3rds

2 quarts water

2 oranges, peeled, thinly sliced

Cooked rice

➤ In 5-quart slow cooker, combine beans, onion, garlic, tomatoes, jalapeño pepper and parsley. Top with Canadian bacon, jerky and sausage. Pour water over all. Cover and cook on LOW 10 to 12 hours or until beans are tender.

➤ With slotted spoon, remove meat from slow cooker. Scoop out about 3 cups beans with liquid. In blender or food processor fitted with metal blade, process these beans until almost smooth. Drain remaining beans; discard liquid.

➤ Combine puréed beans with drained beans. Spoon all beans on large platter. Slice Canadian bacon and sausage. Arrange jerky and sliced meat around side of platter. Serve with sliced oranges and cooked rice.

Each serving contains:

Cal	Prot	Carb	Fat	Chol	Sodium
276	17g	23g	13g	39mg	518mg

New-Style Pozole

Makes 8 to 10 servings

Radishes and avocados lend a delicious potpourri of flavors to this traditional recipe.

1 lb. boneless pork shoulder, cubed

1 lb. chicken thighs

2 slices bacon, chopped

1 small onion, chopped

1/2 teaspoon salt

1 cup chicken broth or bouillon

1 garlic clove, crushed

1 teaspoon chili powder

2 (16-oz.) cans hominy, drained

1/4 teaspoon crushed dried
   red-pepper flakes

Paprika

Sliced radishes

2 avocados, peeled, sliced

➤ In slow cooker, combine all ingredients except paprika, radishes and avocados. Cover and cook on LOW 6 to 7 hours or until meat is tender.

➤ With slotted spoon, remove chicken from pot; remove and discard bones. Cut chicken into slivers; return to pot. Refrigerate. When cold, skim and remove fat.

➤ Just before serving, heat in microwave or on stovetop. Sprinkle with paprika, radishes and avocado.

 In New Mexico, traditional pozole is served on Christmas Eve. Serve with crusty French bread or tortillas.

Each serving contains:

Cal	Prot	Carb	Fat	Chol	Sodium
202	18g	12g	8g	58mg	207mg

Slow-Poke Jambalaya

Makes 7 to 8 servings

Typical flavors of this classic Creole dish have time to mingle in the slow cooker.

1 large red or green bell pepper, seeded, chopped

1 large onion, chopped

2 medium tomatoes, chopped

1 cup chopped celery

1 garlic clove, crushed

2 tablespoons minced fresh parsley

2 teaspoons chopped fresh thyme leaves

2 teaspoons chopped fresh oregano leaves

1/8 teaspoon cayenne

1/2 teaspoon salt

4 oz. smoked sausage, chopped

8 oz. chicken breast, skinned, boned, chopped

2 cups beef broth or bouillon

1/2 lb. cooked, shelled medium shrimp, halved lengthwise

1 cup cooked rice

➤ In slow cooker, combine all ingredients except shrimp and rice. Cover and cook on LOW 9 to 10 hours.

➤ Turn slow cooker on HIGH; add cooked shrimp and cooked rice. Cover; cook on HIGH 20 to 30 minutes.

Each serving contains:

Cal	Prot	Carb	Fat	Chol	Sodium
166	18g	9g	6g	90mg	369mg

Turkey Moussaka Wraps

Makes 8 wraps

Flour tortillas encase this delicious combination.

3/4 lb. ground turkey

1 medium onion, chopped

4 mushrooms, sliced

1 garlic clove, crushed

1 (6-oz.) can tomato paste

1/2 cup dry white wine

1 tablespoon chopped parsley

1/2 teaspoon salt

1 teaspoon pickling spices

4 whole peppercorns

8 flour tortillas

Cucumber Sauce:

1 large cucumber, grated

1 teaspoon chopped fresh mint leaves

1 tablespoon drained capers

1/3 cup milk

1/2 cup unflavored yogurt

1/16 teaspoon ground nutmeg

➤ In slow cooker, combine turkey, onion, mushrooms, garlic, tomato paste, wine, parsley and salt. Tie pickling spices and peppercorns in cheesecloth bag or place them in a tea ball. Add to pot; cover and cook on LOW about 5 hours.

➤ Remove spice bag. Prepare Cucumber Sauce, recipe below.

➤ Spoon about 1/4 cup moussaka onto each tortilla. Top with Cucumber Sauce, fold and wrap, leaving one end open.

Cucumber Sauce: In small bowl, combine all ingredients. Serve over moussaka.

1 wrap contains:

Cal	Prot	Carb	Fat	Chol	Sodium
199	12g	17g	9g	50mg	310mg

Coq Au Vin

Makes about 5 servings

This slow cooker version of the classic French dish of chicken with wine is welcome any time of the year.

1 (2-1/2- to 3-lb.) chicken, cut up	1/8 teaspoon pepper
2 slices bacon, cooked, drained, chopped	15 small white boiling onions
4 shallots, peeled, sliced	10 mushrooms, halved
1 garlic clove, crushed	1/2 cup dry red wine
1 tablespoon chopped fresh parsley	1/2 cup chicken broth or bouillon
1 bay leaf	1 plum tomato, peeled, seeded, finely chopped
1/2 teaspoon chopped fresh thyme	2 tablespoons cornstarch
1/4 teaspoon salt	2 tablespoons cold water

➤ Place chicken in slow cooker. Add cooked bacon, shallots, garlic, parsley, bay leaf, thyme, salt, pepper, onions, mushrooms, wine, broth or bouillon and tomato. Cover and cook on LOW 8 to 9 hours.

➤ Remove chicken and vegetables with slotted spoon. Cover and keep warm. Discard bay leaf. Turn pot on HIGH. Dissolve cornstarch in water; stir into juices in pot. Cover; cook on HIGH 20 to 30 minutes, stirring occasionally. Pour over chicken mixture.

Each serving contains:

Cal	Prot	Carb	Fat	Chol	Sodium
367	47g	10g	13g	136mg	321mg

Tortilla Stack

Makes 6 or 7 servings

Thanks to convenience foods, this delicious-tasting dish is easily put together.

1-1/2 lb. lean ground beef

8 corn tortillas, each cut into
   6 wedges

1 (10-3/4 oz.) can Cheddar cheese
   soup, undiluted

1 pkg. taco seasoning mix (dry)

3 medium tomatoes, chopped

1/4 cup dairy sour cream

2 cups shredded lettuce

1/4 cup chopped green onion

1 red bell pepper, chopped

1 avocado, peeled, chopped

➤ Crumble 1/4 of ground beef into bottom of slow cooker. Top with 1/4 of tortilla wedges.

➤ In small bowl, combine soup and taco mix. Spread 1/4 of soup mixture over tortillas in pot. Sprinkle with 1/4 of tomatoes. Repeat layering until all ingredients are in pot. Cover and cook on LOW 4 to 5 hours.

➤ Spoon onto individual plates. Top each serving with sour cream, shredded lettuce, green onions, bell pepper and avocado.

Each serving contains:

Cal	Prot	Carb	Fat	Chol	Sodium
372	21g	25g	23g	67mg	387mg

Moroccan Hens

Makes 4 servings

For an authentic North African presentation, serve the hens atop the couscous on one large platter.

2 Cornish hens, thawed, halved

1 garlic clove, crushed

1 tablespoon honey

1/4 teaspoon ground turmeric

1 teaspoon grated onion

1/2 teaspoon ground allspice

1/4 teaspoon salt

1/16 teaspoon cayenne

1 large tomato, peeled, seeded, chopped

Cooked couscous or rice

1 tablespoon toasted sesame seeds

➤ Rinse hens; pat dry.

➤ In small bowl, combine garlic, honey, turmeric, onion, allspice, salt and cayenne. Brush on chicken; cover and refrigerate at least 4 hours.

➤ Place in slow cooker with juice from marinade; sprinkle tomatoes over top. Cover; cook on LOW 5-1/2 to 6 hours.

➤ Arrange on serving plate over cooked rice. Sprinkle with toasted sesame seeds.

Each serving contains:

Cal	Prot	Carb	Fat	Chol	Sodium
240	32g	7g	9g	94mg	217mg

Alsatian-Style Choucroute

Makes 6 to 8 servings

The Alsace area of France is where this classic dish originated.

27 to 30 oz. refrigerated or canned sauerkraut

1 medium cooking apple, peeled, seeded, chopped

1 medium onion, chopped

1 carrot, shredded

8 juniper berries

1 bay leaf

1 tablespoon chopped fresh parsley

3 pork chops, boned, halved

6 slices (about 1/2 lb.) Canadian bacon

1/2 lb. smoked sausage, cut into 6 or 8 pieces

1/4 lb. hot Italian sausage, sliced

1/2 cup dry white wine

1 cup chicken broth or bouillon

Cooked new potatoes

➤ Drain sauerkraut in colander or strainer. Rinse; drain again.

➤ In slow cooker, arrange alternate layers of drained sauerkraut, apple, onion and carrot. Tie juniper berries, bay leaf and parsley in cheesecloth; add to pot. Top with pork chops, Canadian bacon, smoked sausage and Italian sausage. Pour wine and chicken broth or bouillon over ingredients in pot. Cover and cook on LOW 6 to 8 hours.

➤ Remove and discard spice bag. With slotted spoon, place sauerkraut and vegetables in center of large platter. Arrange meats over and around vegetables. Serve with cooked new potatoes.

Each serving contains:

Cal	Prot	Carb	Fat	Chol	Sodium
277	19g	9g	17g	63mg	1320mg

Italian-Style Bean Soup

Makes 6 or 7 servings

Although the mushrooms turn dark, you'll enjoy the flavor.

1 cup small dried white beans, rinsed

6 cups chicken broth or bouillon

1 onion, chopped

1/2 cup chopped fennel

1 teaspoon chopped fresh thyme

1 bay leaf

6 mushrooms, coarsely chopped

1/4 teaspoon pepper

2 oz. (about 1/3 cup) prosciutto, chopped

1/4 cup dry white wine

Fennel leaves

➤ In slow cooker, combine beans, broth or bouillon, onion, fennel, thyme, bay leaf, mushrooms, pepper and prosciutto. Cover and cook on LOW 7 to 8 hours or until beans are tender.

➤ Remove and discard bay leaf. Stir in wine. Garnish each serving with a sprig of fennel.

Each serving contains:

Cal	Prot	Carb	Fat	Chol	Sodium
132	11g	16g	2g	5mg	117mg

Crockery Cassoulet

Makes 6 to 7 servings

Mild Italian sausage can be substituted, if you prefer a less spicy dish.

1 lb. dried great Northern beans, rinsed

1 large onion, chopped

1/4 teaspoon pepper

1 garlic clove, crushed

1 tablespoon chopped fresh parsley

2 whole cloves

1 bay leaf

1 sprig fresh thyme

1/4 lb. salt pork, diced

1 lb. boneless lamb, cut into 1-inch cubes

1/2 lb. hot Italian sausage, crumbled

2 medium tomatoes, peeled, seeded, chopped

3 cups beef broth or bouillon

1 cup dry red wine

➤ In slow cooker, combine beans, onion, pepper, garlic and parsley.

➤ Wrap cloves, bay leaf and thyme in cheesecloth or metal tea ball. Add to pot. Add salt pork, lamb, sausage and tomatoes.

➤ Pour beef broth or bouillon and wine over all. Cover; cook on LOW 9 to 10 hours. Remove and discard spice bag.

 Several villages in Southwest France insist they originated Cassoulet (ka su lay). Despite the controversy, most everyone enjoys this hearty dish.

Each serving contains:

Cal	Prot	Carb	Fat	Chol	Sodium
483	39g	31g	20g	92mg	473mg

Slow Cooker and Other Appliances

Wonderful as it is, your slow cooker doesn't replace other appliances. It teams up with them to produce a wide variety of dishes.

Use the microwave for making sauces as well as reheating cooked meat and/or vegetables that are removed before thickening a sauce.

Your oven or toaster oven is handy for toasting nuts, pita rounds and sesame seeds. Pasta and rice can be cooked in a conventional pan on the stovetop before they're drained and added to other ingredients in the slow cooker near the end of cooking.

Turkey Lasagne

Makes 6 to 8 servings

For a lighter dish, I replace beef or sausage with turkey.

3/4 lb. ground turkey

1 small onion, chopped

1/2 cup chopped green or
   red bell pepper

1 garlic clove, crushed

2 (8-oz.) cans tomato sauce

1 (14-1/2-oz.) can ready-cut
   peeled tomatoes

1 teaspoon chicken bouillon
   granules or 1 bouillon cube

1 teaspoon chopped fresh
   oregano leaves

1/4 teaspoon salt

1/8 teaspoon pepper

1/2 lb. lasagne noodles

8 oz. ricotta cheese

8 oz. mozzarella cheese, sliced

➤ In slow cooker, combine turkey, onion, bell pepper, garlic, tomato sauce, tomatoes, bouillon, oregano, salt and pepper. Cover and cook on LOW 7 to 8 hours.

➤ Cook lasagne noodles according to package directions; drain. Preheat oven to 350F (175C).

➤ In 13 by 9-inch baking dish, arrange alternate layers of cooked lasagne noodles, hot turkey-tomato mixture, ricotta cheese and mozzarella cheese. Bake in preheated oven 30 minutes or until bubbly around edges.

Each serving contains:

Cal	Prot	Carb	Fat	Chol	Sodium
324	24g	30g	13g	49mg	830mg

Tropical Baby Back Ribs

Makes 6 to 8 servings

Sesame seeds are the final touch on the spicy-sweet ribs.

1 tablespoon grated fresh
   ginger root

1 garlic clove, crushed

2 tablespoons honey

1/2 teaspoon ground coriander

1/2 teaspoon ground turmeric

1/4 cup soy sauce

2 tablespoons white-wine vinegar

1/4 cup ketchup

1/4 teaspoon salt

4 or 5 drops Tabasco sauce

1 teaspoon instant chicken bouillon or
   1 chicken bouillon cube, crumbled

4 to 5 lb. baby back pork ribs,
   cut into 2- or 3-rib pieces

2 teaspoons sesame seeds

➤ In small bowl, combine ginger root, garlic, honey, coriander, turmeric, soy sauce, vinegar, ketchup, salt, Tabasco sauce and bouillon.

➤ Brush both sides of ribs with sauce. Place in slow cooker. Pour remaining sauce over all. Cover and cook on LOW 6 to 7 hours or until tender.

➤ With fork or slotted spoon, lift ribs from slow cooker. Place single layer of drained ribs in shallow baking pan; brush with drippings in pot. Sprinkle with sesame seeds. Broil in oven until sesame seeds begin to brown.

Each serving contains:

Cal	Prot	Carb	Fat	Chol	Sodium
375	26g	8g	26g	103mg	891mg

Southwestern Sauce

Makes about 2-3/4 cups sauce

You'll find many uses for this simple, versatile sauce.

4 medium tomatoes, peeled, seeded, chopped

3 medium tomatillos, husked, chopped

1 tablespoon vegetable oil

1 tablespoon minced green onions

1 jalapeño pepper, seeded, chopped

1 garlic clove, crushed

1 tablespoon red-wine vinegar

1 tablespoon chopped fresh cilantro

1/4 teaspoon salt

Broiled fish or chicken

Fresh cilantro leaves

➤ In 1-quart slow cooker, combine tomatoes, tomatillos, oil, onions, jalapeño pepper, garlic, vinegar, 1 tablespoon cilantro and salt. Cover and cook on LOW 3-1/2 to 4 hours.

➤ Spoon over broiled fish or chicken. Garnish with cilantro leaves.

 Use this sauce to add zest to beans or spice up roast beef or lamb sandwiches.

1 tablespoon contains:

Cal	Prot	Carb	Fat	Chol	Sodium
7	0g	1g	0g	0mg	17mg

Stuffed Onions

Makes 5 servings

These stuffed onions are made Southeast-Asia style. Use the onion centers to season other vegetable or meat dishes.

5 medium onions, peeled
1/2 lb. ground turkey
1/2 cup soft breadcrumbs
1 egg, beaten slightly
1 garlic clove, crushed
1 tablespoon soy sauce
1 tablespoon hoisin sauce
1/4 teaspoon ground ginger

Plum Glaze:
1/2 cup plum jelly
1 tablespoon white-wine vinegar
1 tablespoon ketchup
1 teaspoon Dijon-style mustard
Toasted sesame seeds

➤ With sharp knife, cut about 1/2-inch slice across top of each onion. Carefully cut out centers, leaving about 1/2-inch sides and bottom.

➤ In medium bowl, combine turkey, breadcrumbs, egg, garlic, soy sauce, hoisin sauce and ginger. Spoon about 1/4 cup stuffing into each onion shell.

➤ Place rack in slow cooker, add 1/2 cup water. Arrange filled onions on rack. If all onions do not fit on bottom of cooker, place 3 on bottom; lightly cover with heavy-duty foil. Arrange remaining onions on top. Cover and cook on LOW 7 to 8 hours or until onions are tender. Spoon Plum Glaze over onions.

Plum Glaze: At serving time, combine jelly, vinegar, ketchup and mustard. Stir over low heat or heat in microwave until dissolved. Spoon over cooked onions. Sprinkle with sesame seeds.

Each serving contains:

Cal	Prot	Carb	Fat	Chol	Sodium
219	12g	29g	7g	69mg	380mg

Refried Beans (Frijoles)

Makes 7-1/2 cups

Frijoles are a great accompaniment to enchiladas, tacos or other Mexican dishes, as well as chicken or steak.

1 lb. dried pinto beans, rinsed	6 cups water
1/4 teaspoon dried red-pepper flakes	1/2 teaspoon salt, optional
1 garlic clove	1 tablespoon vegetable oil
1/4 lb. salt pork, cubed	Shredded Cheddar cheese, optional

➤ In slow cooker, combine dried beans, red-pepper flakes, garlic, salt pork and water. Cover and cook on LOW 10 to 11 hours. Add salt, if desired.

➤ Partially mash beans with potato masher or in food processor. Serve now or refrigerate.

➤ Just before serving, heat oil in large skillet. Add beans; heat and stir until fairly dry. Top with cheese or serve plain.

1 cup contains:

Cal	Prot	Carb	Fat	Chol	Sodium
226	12g	31g	6g	6mg	123mg

Stuffed Acorn Squash

Makes 4 servings

Depending on how spicy you like your food, use hot or regular sausage.

2 acorn squash, halved, seeded

1 tablespoon vegetable oil

1/2 lb. bulk sausage

1 egg, beaten slightly

3 slices raisin bread, toasted,
    coarsely crumbled

1/4 teaspoon ground nutmeg

1/2 teaspoon Dijon-style mustard

1 orange, peeled, cut into
    4 crosswise slices

Orange-Nutmeg Sauce:

1 tablespoon cornstarch

1 cup orange juice

1 tablespoon honey

1 teaspoon lemon juice

Ground nutmeg

➤ Brush cut edges and inside squash with oil.

➤ In small bowl, combine sausage, egg, toasted bread, nutmeg and mustard. Spoon into squash halves.

➤ Place cut-side up on rack in slow cooker. Top each with slice of orange. Cover pot, cook on LOW 5 to 6 hours or until squash is tender. Spoon Orange-Nutmeg Sauce over all.

Orange-Nutmeg Sauce: In small saucepan or microwave dish, dissolve cornstarch in orange juice. Cook over moderate heat or in microwave until thickened. Stir in honey and lemon juice. Spoon over cooked squash. Sprinkle with nutmeg.

Each serving contains:

Cal	Prot	Carb	Fat	Chol	Sodium
529	13g	60g	29g	92mg	481mg

Curried Carrot Bisque

Makes about 6 cups

An appetizing golden color plus mouth-watering flavors guarantee a hit.

8 medium carrots, peeled, chopped

1 onion, chopped

1 tart apple, peeled, chopped

1 teaspoon curry powder

1 garlic clove, crushed

1/4 teaspoon ground coriander

1/8 teaspoon allspice

1/4 teaspoon salt

3 cups chicken broth or bouillon

1 cup milk or light cream

Chopped fresh cilantro leaves

➤ In slow cooker, combine carrots, onion, apple, curry powder, garlic, coriander, allspice, salt and broth or bouillon. Cover and cook on LOW 9 to 10 hours or until carrots are very tender.

➤ Purée, half at a time, in blender or food processor fitted with metal blade. Gradually stir in milk or cream. Reheat in microwave or in saucepan on stove. Sprinkle cilantro on top.

 Although there is an herb that's called curry plant, the curry powder we're familiar with is a blend of many spices. Turmeric supplies the deep golden color.

1 cup contains:

Cal	Prot	Carb	Fat	Chol	Sodium
98	5g	16g	2g	4mg	143mg

Turkey Stew

Makes 8 to 9 servings

The Baked Cheddar Topping featured in this recipe is also delicious on Barbecued Beans 'n' Beef, page 141, or Beef 'n' Turkey-Sausage Chili, page 33.

1 lb. dried black-eye peas, rinsed

2 cups chicken broth or bouillon

4 cups water

1 teaspoon ground coriander

1/2 teaspoon ground cumin

1 teaspoon ground cardamom

1 onion, chopped

1/8 teaspoon dried red-pepper flakes, crushed

1/2 teaspoon salt

2 (about 1-1/2-lb.) turkey thighs, skinned

Baked Cheddar Topping:

1-1/2 cups boiling water

1/4 teaspoon salt

2/3 cup yellow cornmeal

1 egg, beaten slightly

4 tablespoons dairy sour cream

3/4 cup shredded Cheddar cheese

➤ In slow cooker, combine dried peas, broth or bouillon and water. Stir in coriander, cumin, cardamom, onion, red-pepper flakes and salt. Place turkey pieces on top of dried peas and seasonings. Cover and cook on LOW 9 to 10 hours or until peas are tender.

➤ Remove turkey; cut meat into small chunks or shreds. Discard bones. Place meat and stew in casserole. Prepare Baked Cheddar Topping.

Baked Cheddar Topping: In medium saucepan, combine water and salt; gradually stir in cornmeal. Cook, stirring constantly, about 5 minutes or until thick. Remove from heat. Preheat oven to 375F (190C). Mix egg, sour cream and cheese. Gradually stir in cooked cornmeal. Drop in 9 mounds on top of cooked mixture in casserole.

➤ Bake casserole 25 to 35 minutes or until topping begins to brown.

Each serving contains:

Cal	Prot	Carb	Fat	Chol	Sodium
296	24g	30g	9g	69mg	280mg

Greek Isles Pita Pockets, page 96

Hot Baja Coffee, page 144

Mixed Vegetable Purée

Makes 6 servings

This purée is perfect to prepare the day before, then heat in the oven just before serving.

5 medium potatoes, peeled, quartered

1 medium celery root, peeled, cubed

1 medium leek, trimmed, cut into 1/2-inch crosswise slices

1 garlic clove, minced

2 tablespoons chopped sun-dried tomatoes

1/2 teaspoon salt

1/8 teaspoon pepper

1/4 teaspoon seasoned salt

4 cups water

1/2 cup milk or half-and-half

1 egg, slightly beaten

1 tablespoon minced parsley

1/4 cup melted margarine or butter

➤ In slow cooker, combine potatoes, celery root, leek, garlic, sun-dried tomatoes, salt, pepper, seasoned salt and water. Cover and cook on LOW 6 to 7 hours or until tender.

➤ Drain; mash with electric mixer or food processor fitted with metal blade. Add milk or half-and-half, egg, parsley and 3 tablespoons melted margarine or butter.

➤ Spoon into a buttered 1-1/2-quart baking dish. Drizzle top with remaining tablespoon of melted margarine or butter. Bake in preheated 350F (175C) oven 25 to 30 minutes or until slightly browned on top.

Each serving contains:

Cal	Prot	Carb	Fat	Chol	Sodium
197	5g	30g	7g	37mg	456mg

Almond Ginger Apples

Makes 6 servings

Apples never had it so good! Try it and you'll agree.

6 large apples

1/4 cup almond paste

2 tablespoons powdered sugar

1 tablespoon minced crystallized ginger

1/4 teaspoon grated lemon peel

1/4 cup chopped toasted almonds

1 egg white

1/8 teaspoon lemon juice

1 tablespoon granulated sugar

2 tablespoons slivered almonds

➤ With vegetable peeler, remove apple cores. In small bowl, combine almond paste, powdered sugar, ginger, lemon peel and chopped almonds. Spoon into center of each apple.

➤ Place in slow cooker. If all apples do not fit on bottom of cooker, place 3 on bottom; lightly cover with heavy-duty foil. Arrange remaining apples on top of foil. Cover and cook on LOW 4 to 5 hours or until apples are done.

➤ Just before serving, in small mixing bowl, beat egg white and lemon juice until foamy. Gradually beat in granulated sugar until peaks are stiff but not dry. Swirl on top of cooked apples. Place apples in broiler pan; sprinkle with slivered almonds. Broil until brown on top. Serve immediately. Spoon juice from slow cooker over top, if desired.

 The meringue topping makes an interesting presentation but may be omitted, if desired.

Each serving contains:

Cal	Prot	Carb	Fat	Chol	Sodium
182	3g	30g	7g	0mg	11mg

Cook Today—
Serve Tomorrow

Because some foods take all day or night to cook, it's important to consider when to start the cooking process. You don't want to get out of bed in the middle of the night to turn off the pot.

Foods in this chapter are cooked, then chilled before serving. That's a good reason to let them cook one day, then refrigerate overnight for serving the next day. Summertime menus can be enhanced with these cold soups and main-dish salads.

Cranberry-Ginger Chutney

Makes bout 3-1/2 cups

Dried apples or dates can be substituted for the raisins.

6 oz. fresh cranberries

2 tablespoons chopped crystallized ginger

1/2 cup chopped onion

1 teaspoon lemon juice

1 teaspoon grated lemon peel

1/2 teaspoon ground cinnamon

2 apples, peeled, cored, chopped

1/2 cup chopped dried apricots

1/2 cup raisins

1/3 cup red wine

1/3 cup rice-wine or cider vinegar

1/2 cup sugar

5 tablespoons brown sugar

1/3 cup chopped walnuts

1/4 red pepper flakes

Place all ingredients in a slow cooker. Cover and cook on LOW 5 to 6 hours.

Each serving contains:

Cal	Prot	Carb	Fat	Chol	Sodium
85	1g	18g	1g	0mg	2mg

Emerald-Green Vichyssoise

Makes 8 servings

Plan ahead for adequate time to refrigerate this dish several hours or overnight.

5 medium potatoes, peeled,
  cut into 8ths

2 leeks, washed, sliced crosswise

1/4 cup fresh basil leaves

1 (10-oz.) pkg. frozen chopped
  spinach, thawed, drained

1/4 cup watercress leaves

3 cups chicken broth or bouillon

1/2 teaspoon seasoned salt

2 cups milk

1/2 teaspoon salt

1/8 teaspoon pepper

1 cup light cream

Fresh basil springs for garnish

➤ In slow cooker, combine potatoes, leeks, basil, spinach, watercress, broth or bouillon, seasoned salt, milk, salt and pepper. Cover and cook on LOW 6 to 7 hours or until vegetables are very tender.

➤ Purée in blender or food processor fitted with metal blade. Add light cream; refrigerate until cold.

➤ Ladle into individual bowls. Garnish with basil sprigs.

 Spinach and watercress supply both color and flavor.

Each serving contains:

Cal	Prot	Carb	Fat	Chol	Sodium
206	8g	28g	8g	26mg	283mg

Cool Curry Soup

Makes about 6 cups

This wonderful warm-weather dish is smooth, cool and flavorful.

3 apples, peeled, cored, chopped

6 carrots, peeled, chopped

1 small onion, chopped

1 tablespoon margarine or butter

2 teaspoons curry powder

1/8 teaspoon ground allspice

1/4 teaspoon salt

1/8 teaspoon pepper

3 cups chicken broth or bouillon

1/2 cup dairy sour cream

2 tablespoons toasted slivered almonds

➤ In slow cooker, combine apples, carrots, onions, margarine or butter, curry powder, allspice, salt, pepper and broth or bouillon. Cover and cook on LOW 9 to 10 hours or until vegetables are very soft.

➤ Purée half at a time, in blender or food processor fitted with metal blade. Refrigerate at least 3 hours or until chilled. Stir in sour cream. Sprinkle with toasted almonds.

 Cook this soup the night before, refrigerate all day, then serve cold for dinner.

1 cup contains:

Cal	Prot	Carb	Fat	Chol	Sodium
161	5g	20g	8g	9mg	148mg

Summer Squash Soup

Makes 6 servings

A refreshing cold soup to make when summer squash is at the peak of garden-fresh flavor.

3 medium crookneck squash, sliced

3 medium zucchini, sliced

2 tablespoons sliced green onions

1 garlic clove, crushed

1/2 teaspoon salt

1/8 teaspoon pepper

3 cups chicken broth or bouillon

1/4 cup loosely packed watercress leaves

1/2 cup plain lowfat yogurt, stirred

1/4 teaspoon dried dill weed

Watercress sprigs for garnish

➤ In slow cooker, combine crookneck squash, zucchini, green onions, garlic, salt, pepper and broth or bouillon. Cover and cook on LOW 7 to 8 hours or until squash is very tender.

➤ In blender or food processor fitted with metal blade, purée hot vegetable mixture with watercress, yogurt and dill until smooth.

➤ Chill several hours or overnight. Serve in individual bowls; garnish with watercress sprigs.

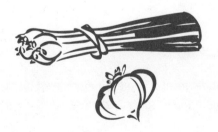

Each serving contains:

Cal	Prot	Carb	Fat	Chol	Sodium
50	4g	6g	1g	2mg	194mg

Barbecued Beef Sandwiches

Makes 10 to 12 servings

Good ol' barbecued beef sandwiches—always a hit, no matter what time of the year.

2-1/2 to 3 lb. lean boneless
   chuck roast

3/4 cup tomato ketchup

1 tablespoon Dijon-style mustard

2 tablespoons brown sugar

1 garlic clove, crushed

1 tablespoon Worcestershire sauce

2 tablespoons red-wine vinegar

1/4 teaspoon liquid-smoke flavoring

1/4 teaspoon salt

1/8 teaspoon pepper

10 to 12 French rolls or sandwich
   buns

➤ Place beef in slow cooker. Combine remaining ingredients, except rolls. Pour over meat. Cover and cook on LOW 8 to 9 hours.

➤ Refrigerate or prepare sandwiches now. Shred beef by pulling it apart with 2 forks; add 1 cup sauce. Reheat mixture in microwave or on stovetop.

➤ Spoon on warm, open-face rolls or buns. Top with additional warm sauce, if desired.

 If the meat is cooked a day ahead and refrigerated overnight, skim solidified fat from top of sauce and meat. Then, shred beef, reheat and spoon onto rolls.

Each serving contains:

Cal	Prot	Carb	Fat	Chol	Sodium
420	29g	42g	14g	75mg	711mg

Smoked Turkey & Bean Salad

Makes 6 or 7 servings

For an inviting summer lunch, add a crunchy French roll and a glass of iced tea.

1 cup dried pinto beans, rinsed

1 cup dried garbanzo beans, rinsed

1/4 lb. smoked turkey, diced

4 cups water

2 tablespoons chopped fresh parsley

1 garlic clove, crushed

1 cup cooked green beans, drained

1/2 cup olive oil

1/4 cup white-wine vinegar

1 tablespoon Dijon-style mustard

2 teaspoons honey

2 tablespoons chopped fresh chives

1/2 teaspoon dried dill weed

1/4 teaspoon salt

1/8 teaspoon pepper

1 small cucumber, peeled, diced

1/4 cup loosely packed watercress leaves

Lettuce

Chopped pimiento

➤ In slow cooker, combine dried beans, turkey, water, parsley and garlic. Cover; cook on LOW 10 to 11 hours or until beans are tender but firm.

➤ Drain and discard liquid; cool drained bean mixture. Add green beans.

➤ In medium bowl, combine oil, vinegar, mustard, honey, chives, dill, salt and pepper. Pour over bean mixture; chill. Stir in cucumber and watercress.

➤ Serve in lettuce-lined bowl. Sprinkle with chopped pimiento.

Each serving contains:

Cal	Prot	Carb	Fat	Chol	Sodium
319	12g	30g	18g	7mg	277mg

Antipasto Bean Salad

Makes 7 to 8 servings

Turn a side dish into a main dish by serving with sliced salami and mortadella, plus a loaf of Italian bread.

1 lb. dried pink beans, rinsed

6 cups chicken broth or bouillon

1 garlic clove, crushed

1/4 cup chopped celery leaves

1/2 cup olive oil

1/4 cup vegetable oil

1/3 cup white-wine vinegar

1/4 cup loosely packed chopped basil

4 anchovy filets, chopped

1 red onion, thinly sliced

2 medium tomatoes, chopped

1/4 cup sliced ripe olives

1/2 teaspoon salt

1/8 teaspoon pepper

Lettuce leaves

1/4 cup (1 oz.) Gorgonzola cheese, crumbled

➤ The day before serving, combine dried beans, broth or bouillon, garlic and celery leaves in slow cooker. Cover and cook on LOW 9 to 10 hours or until beans are tender.

➤ Drain; refrigerate beans several hours or overnight. Discard liquid.

➤ In large bowl, toss chilled beans with oils, vinegar, basil, anchovies, onions, tomatoes, olives, salt and pepper. Spoon into lettuce-lined bowls or plates. Sprinkle with Gorgonzola cheese.

Each serving contains:

Cal	Prot	Carb	Fat	Chol	Sodium
398	15g	33g	24g	6mg	311mg

Pinto Pepper Salad

Makes 7 or 8 servings

Have you ever had a cold bean salad? Then try this colorful salad that never fails to win admiration.

1 lb. dried pinto beans, rinsed	2 cups cherry tomatoes, halved
6 cups water	1 cup thinly sliced fennel
1 yellow or green bell pepper, seeded, chopped	1/2 cup bottled Italian salad dressing
1 fresh mild green chile or jalapeño pepper, seeded, finely chopped	Lettuce
1 small red onion, diced	Hard-cooked eggs

➤ In slow cooker, combine dried beans and water. Cover and cook on LOW 9 to 10 hours or until beans are done.

➤ Remove beans with slotted spoon; discard liquid and refrigerate beans until chilled.

➤ In large bowl, combine drained beans, bell pepper, chile or jalapeño pepper, onion, tomatoes and fennel. Add salad dressing; toss. Serve on lettuce; garnish with wedges of hard-cooked eggs.

Each serving contains:

Cal	Prot	Carb	Fat	Chol	Sodium
449	10g	39g	36g	0mg	482mg

Black Bean Vinaigrette

Makes 6 to 8 servings

When shopping, try to find meaty ham hocks with a minimum of fat.

1 lb. dried black beans, rinsed

7 cups water

2 ham hocks or 1 cup chopped ham

1 garlic clove, crushed

2 fresh jalapeño peppers, seeded, chopped

3/4 cup olive or vegetable oil

1/3 cup red-wine vinegar

1/2 cup chopped red or yellow bell pepper

2 tablespoons chopped fresh parsley

1/4 cup chopped green onion

1/2 teaspoon salt

2 tablespoons capers

Lettuce leaves

2 hard-cooked eggs, chopped

➤ The day before serving, combine dried beans, water, ham, garlic and jalapeño peppers in slow cooker. Cover and cook on LOW 8 to 9 hours or until beans are tender. Cool to room temperature or refrigerate overnight.

➤ Drain thoroughly; discard liquid. If using ham hocks, chop lean meat; discard bones, skin and fat.

➤ In small bowl, combine oil, vinegar, bell pepper, parsley, green onion, salt and capers. Pour over beans; toss. Spoon into lettuce-lined bowl. Sprinkle chopped eggs on top.

 Black beans, also called turtle beans, *are a staple in Mexico and countries to the south.*

Each serving contains:

Cal	Prot	Carb	Fat	Chol	Sodium
397	16g	29g	25g	64mg	435mg

Tunisian Eggplant Dip

Makes 3-1/4 cups dip

If you're short of time, substitute packaged tortilla chips for pita or tortillas.

2 medium eggplants, peeled, cubed

1/4 cup sun-dried tomatoes in oil, drained, chopped

1 garlic clove, crushed

1 onion, chopped

1 tablespoon chopped fresh Italian parsley

1/2 teaspoon chopped fresh thyme

1 tablespoon vegetable oil

1/2 teaspoon salt

1/4 teaspoon pepper

1/4 teaspoon crushed, dried red-pepper flakes

1/2 cup plain yogurt

2 teaspoons toasted sesame seeds

1/4 cup sliced ripe olives

Wedges of toasted pita rounds or corn tortillas

➤ In slow cooker, combine eggplants, tomatoes, garlic, onion, parsley, thyme, oil, salt, pepper and red-pepper flakes. Cover and cook on LOW 6 or 7 hours or until vegetables are soft.

➤ With slotted spoon, scoop eggplant mixture into blender or food processor fitted with metal blade. Process until smooth. Stir in yogurt.

➤ Spoon into shallow bowl; sprinkle with sesame seeds. Garnish with olives. Scoop on wedges of toasted pita bread or tortillas.

1 tablespoon contains:

Cal	Prot	Carb	Fat	Chol	Sodium
14	0g	2g	1g	0mg	28mg

Farmer's Pride Relish

Makes about 3-1/2 cups

If fresh corn is not available, use 2/3 cup frozen kernels and enjoy this old-time relish any time of the year.

2 ears corn

1 large green or red bell pepper, seeded, coarsely chopped

1 onion, chopped

2 cups thinly sliced cabbage

1/2 teaspoon dried red-pepper flakes

2/3 cup white-wine vinegar

1/3 cup sugar

1/2 teaspoon curry powder

1/2 teaspoon ground coriander

1/4 teaspoon ground turmeric

1 teaspoon dry mustard

1/2 teaspoon salt

➤ Cut corn off cob. Combine in slow cooker with bell pepper, onion, cabbage, red-pepper flakes, vinegar, sugar, curry powder, coriander, turmeric, dry mustard and salt. Cover; cook on LOW 6 to 7 hours.

➤ Cool and serve as an accompaniment to chicken or pork.

1 tablespoon contains:

Cal	Prot	Carb	Fat	Chol	Sodium
9	0g	2g	0g	0mg	20mg

Winter Chutney

Makes about 3 cups

An unusual accompaniment to roast duck, chicken or pork.

3 firm pears, peeled, seeded, cut into chunks

1 cup dried fruit bits

2 tablespoons sliced green onion

2 tablespoons lemon juice

1 cup sugar

1 teaspoon grated lemon peel

1/4 teaspoon crushed dried red-pepper flakes

1-1/2 teaspoon slivered crystallized ginger

➤ In slow cooker, combine pears, dried fruit, green onions, lemon juice, sugar, lemon peel, red-pepper flakes and ginger. Cover and cook on LOW 3 to 4 hours. Cool.

 Chutney is a relish that originated in East India. It usually combines sweet and sour ingredients. Both fruits and vegetables are teamed with herbs, spices and other seasonings.

1 tablespoon contains:

Cal	Prot	Carb	Fat	Chol	Sodium
28	0g	7g	0g	0mg	1mg

Quick and Easy

If you're like most of us—so busy getting the family off to school and work that there's practically no time left to make dinner preparations—then this chapter is designed for you.

With the availability of convenience foods, much of the tedious work is done for you. A package of pork chops or chicken pieces turns into a culinary marvel with very little time and effort on your part. These recipes take the normal amount of cooking time in a slow cooker, but the preparation time is shorter than usual.

Shortcut Spareribs

Makes 4 to 6 servings

For a more crispy texture, place single layer of cooked and drained ribs in shallow baking pan; broil in oven until brown on edges.

3 to 4 lb. pork spareribs

1 cup bottled barbecue sauce

1 (1/2-oz.) pkg. dry green-onion-dip mix

➤ Cut spareribs into individual ribs; place in slow cooker.

➤ Combine barbecue sauce and green-onion-dip mix. Spoon over ribs. Cover and cook on LOW 6 to 7 hours or until ribs are tender. With fork or slotted spoon, lift ribs to platter.

Each serving contains:

Cal	Prot	Carb	Fat	Chol	Sodium
494	34g	7g	36g	137mg	953mg

Tender Tasty Fajitas

Makes 6 or 7 servings

If you prefer poultry, substitute 1 to 1-1/2 lb. chicken or turkey, skinned and boned, for the beef.

1 to 1-1/2 lb. boneless beef round steak, cut in strips

1 red bell pepper, cut in strips

1 large onion, cut into thin wedges

1 (1-oz.) pkg. dry fajita mix

1/4 cup water

6 or 7 (7- or 8-inch) flour tortillas

2 small tomatoes, chopped

1 avocado, peeled, thinly sliced

1/2 cup dairy sour cream

➤ In slow cooker, combine beef, bell pepper, onion, fajita mix and water. Cover and cook on LOW 5 to 6 hours or until meat is tender.

➤ Warm tortillas in microwave or conventional oven.

➤ With slotted spoon, lift meat mixture out of pot. Place about 3/4 cup mixture along center of each tortilla. Top with chopped tomato, avocado and sour cream. Fold both sides over filling.

 Don't expect these fajitas to be sizzling and crunchy brown like those in many restaurants. But the flavor is outstanding!

Each serving contains:

Cal	Prot	Carb	Fat	Chol	Sodium
292	19g	22g	15g	54mg	155mg

Sweet-Sour Pork Chops

Makes 6 servings

Chicken breasts can be substituted for pork in this quick-to-fix dish.

1 (16-oz.) bag frozen Oriental-style
  vegetables, partially thawed

6 (about 2-1/4 lb.) pork chops

1 (2-oz.) pkg. sweet-sour sauce
  blend mix

1/2 cup water

1 cup Chinese pea pods

1 (9-oz.) can pineapple chunks,
  drained

➤ Place partially thawed vegetables in slow cooker. Arrange pork chops on top.
Combine sauce mix and water. Pour sauce over chops and vegetables in slow
cooker. Cover and cook on LOW 7 to 8 hours.

➤ Turn on HIGH; add pea pods and pineapple. Cover and cook on HIGH about
5 minutes.

Each serving contains:

Cal	Prot	Carb	Fat	Chol	Sodium
205	21g	12g	8g	58mg	69mg

Potato-Leek Chicken Thighs

Makes 5 to 6 servings

Delicate leek and pimiento flavors highlight an unusual chicken main dish.

5 medium potatoes, peeled, sliced	10 to 12 chicken thighs
1 medium leek, washed, thinly sliced	1 (1.8-oz.) pkg. leek soup mix
1 (2-oz.) jar pimiento strips, drained	1 cup cold water

➤ Combine potatoes, leek and pimiento. Place on bottom of slow cooker. Arrange chicken over potatoes.

➤ In small bowl, combine leek soup mix and water. Whisk until well mixed. Pour over chicken. Cover; cook on LOW 5 to 6 hours or until chicken is tender. Serve with sliced tomatoes and hot biscuits.

Each serving contains:

Cal	Prot	Carb	Fat	Chol	Sodium
442	34g	30g	20g	116mg	874mg

Sunshine Drumsticks

Makes 12 drumsticks

Add one (8-oz.) can drained mandarin oranges to cooked sauce for a more pronounced citrus flavor.

12 chicken drumsticks, skinned

1 (6-oz. or 12-oz.) can frozen orange juice concentrate, thawed, not reconstituted

2 to 3 tablespoons honey

2 tablespoons quick-cooking tapioca

1 fresh mild green chile or jalapeño pepper, seeded, thinly sliced

1/4 teaspoon salt

1 teaspoon dried onion flakes

➤ Place chicken in slow cooker.

➤ In small bowl, combine orange juice concentrate, honey, tapioca, chile or jalapeño pepper, salt and onions. Pour over chicken. Cover and cook on LOW about 5 hours or until tender. Spoon sauce over chicken.

 Adjust the flavorings to your personal taste. Use the higher range of orange juice, honey or jalapeño for extra orange flavor, sweetness or spice.

1 drumstick contains:

Cal	Prot	Carb	Fat	Chol	Sodium
152	15g	12g	6g	48mg	92mg

Honey-Mustard Barbecued Short Ribs

Makes 6 to 8 servings

Long slow cooking is required to make meaty short ribs tender and juicy.

3 to 3-1/2 lb. beef short ribs
1 tablespoon Dijon-style mustard
1 garlic clove, crushed
2 tablespoons honey
1/2 teaspoon salt
1/8 teaspoon pepper

1 cup bottled hickory smoke
　barbecue sauce
2 tablespoons cornstarch
2 tablespoons cold water
Cooked noodles

➤ Place short ribs in slow cooker.

➤ In medium bowl, combine mustard, garlic, honey, salt, pepper and barbecue
sauce. Pour over ribs. Cover and cook on LOW 6 to 7 hours or until tender.
Refrigerate several hours or overnight. Skim solidified fat from top.

➤ Remove ribs; heat in microwave or conventional oven. Dissolve cornstarch
in cold water. Add to sauce from ribs. Cook and stir in microwave or on
stovetop until hot and slightly thickened. Pour hot sauce over warm ribs.
Serve on cooked noodles.

Each serving contains:

Cal	Prot	Carb	Fat	Chol	Sodium
349	35g	9g	18g	102mg	507mg

Barbecued Beans 'n' Beef

Makes 6 to 8 servings

Your family or friends will never guess you used canned beans and bottled barbecue sauce to make this delicious barbecue dish.

1-1/2 lb. round steak or beef stew meat, cut into 1/2-inch cubes

1 onion, chopped

1/2 cup finely chopped celery

1 yellow or green bell pepper, seeded, chopped

2 (15-oz.) cans pinto beans, drained

1/4 teaspoon salt

1 cup bottled hickory smoke barbecue sauce

1 cup (4 oz.) grated Cheddar cheese, optional

In slow cooker, combine all ingredients except cheese. Cover; cook on LOW 7 to 8 hours or until meat is tender. Top with grated cheese, if desired.

Each serving contains:

Cal	Prot	Carb	Fat	Chol	Sodium
314	30g	32g	8g	61mg	363mg

Picante Tomato Drink

Makes 9 or 10 servings

Choose either mild or hot picante sauce, depending on how much "heat" you can stand.

1 (8-oz.) jar picante sauce	2 quarts tomato juice
1/4 cup loosely packed cilantro leaves	2 cups beef broth or bouillon

➤ In blender or food processor fitted with metal blade, combine picante sauce and cilantro. Process until smooth.

➤ Pour into slow cooker with tomato juice and broth or bouillon. Cover; cook on LOW 4 to 5 hours. Stir well; serve in mugs or coffee cups.

 A warm spicy drink, ideal for warming up on those cold days.

Each serving contains:

Cal	Prot	Carb	Fat	Chol	Sodium
46	2g	9g	1g	0mg	728mg

"No Chopping" Vegetable Soup

Makes 7 to 8 servings

Stir-fry strips of pork or beef can be substituted for the turkey.

2 cups beef broth or bouillon

1 (14-oz.) can stewed tomatoes

1 (16-oz.) can kidney beans, drained

1 (10-oz.) pkg. frozen mixed vegetables

1 (10-oz.) pkg. frozen baby onions

1 lb. fresh boneless turkey strips

1 teaspoon chili powder

1/2 teaspoon salt

1/8 teaspoon pepper

1 cup crushed tortilla chips

➤ In slow cooker, combine all ingredients except tortilla chips. Cover; cook on LOW 8 or 9 hours or until vegetables are done.

➤ Serve in individual bowls; sprinkle with tortilla chips.

Each serving contains:

Cal	Prot	Carb	Fat	Chol	Sodium
217	23g	22g	4g	39mg	497mg

Hot Baja Coffee

Makes 10 to 12 servings

This delightful drink is good enough to be called dessert. For a festive touch, add cinnamon sticks for stirring.

8 cups hot water

3 tablespoons instant coffee granules

1/2 cup coffee liqueur

1/4 cup crème de cacao liqueur

3/4 cup whipped cream

2 tablespoons grated semi-sweet chocolate

➤ In slow cooker, combine hot water, coffee granules and liqueurs. Cover and heat on LOW 2 to 4 hours.

➤ Ladle into mugs or heat-proof glasses. Top with whipped cream and grated chocolate.

Each serving contains:

Cal	Prot	Carb	Fat	Chol	Sodium
98	0g	9g	3g	10mg	10mg

Double-Corn Dumplings

An old-fashioned comfort food you can add to other dishes.

3/4 cup all-purpose flour

1/4 cup yellow cornmeal

2 teaspoons baking powder

1/8 teaspoon salt

1/2 cup fresh corn kernels

1/2 cup milk

2 tablespoons vegetable oil

1 tablespoon chopped fresh cilantro
or chives

➤ In medium bowl, combine flour, cornmeal, baking powder and salt. Stir in corn, milk, oil and cilantro or chives.

➤ Spoon on cooked hot stew or chili in slow cooker. Cover and cook on HIGH 30 to 35 minutes.

Each serving contains:

Cal	Prot	Carb	Fat	Chol	Sodium
85	2g	12g	3g	1mg	100mg

Index